ALIENS

Jenny Randles has been a professional ufologist for almost twenty years and has researched innumerable bizarre cases on four continents. She has worked with some of the most respected associations in her field. She is British representative for America's most prestigious UFO investigation group, the Dr J. Allen Hynek Center for UFO Studies. For six years she has written and presented UFO Call, a weekly news and information service, and is consultant to the television series *Strange but True*. She is the author of many books including *Spontaneous Human Combustion*, *The Paranormal Year* and *Crop Circles*, all published by Hale. Jenny Randles lives in Cheshire.

By Jenny Randles

Beyond Explanation?
Abduction
Phantoms of the Soap Operas
The Paranormal Year: 1993 Edition

With Paul Fuller

Crop Circles: A Mystery Solved

With Peter Hough

Spontaneous Human Combustion

ALIENS
The Real Story

Jenny Randles

ROBERT HALE · LONDON

ISBN 0 7090 5567 6

Robert Hale Limited
Clerkenwell House
Clerkenwell Green
London EC1R 0HT

1   3   5   7   9   10   8   6   4   2

Printed and bound in Malta by Interprint Limited

Contents

PART ONE

The History of Alien Contact

Introduction

A Century of Aliens

For many years, perhaps throughout much of history, mankind has shared this world with other intelligent beings. That seems to be the conclusion many draw from stories handed down across the generations. Every race and culture has its own history and traditions of such strange entities.

In the Bible we find the *Elohim*, mysterious beings who occasionally interact with the world of mortals, riding 'cloud ships' and possessed with incredible powers. On the whole there were two types of 'angel' (another term since adopted for these beings). In effect they were the 'goodies' and the 'baddies'. Both treated humans as somewhat inferior, at best being indifferent and at worst rather meddlesome. But it was believed that overall they had the interests of humanity at heart.

Such elemental beings have formed a backdrop to the religion and folklore of all nations for some millenia. In the east they are called 'djinns' – where our romantic image of the magical 'genie' derives from. Elsewhere they may go by many different names, but the consistency between belief in such entities is truly remarkable.

There is also another kind of elemental which peppers the folk history of most races. These are not described as tall, supernatural and magical in tone with a reasonably benevolent nature towards us. Instead, they are small, often dwarf-like, and can be aggressively unconcerned as regards to what they do to unfortunate earth dwellers who chance to get in their way.

Folklorists the world over know about 'the little people'. Their names are many. The *trolls* of Scandinavia, the *ihkals* of Mexico and central America, the *fions* of northern France, the *bunians* of Malaysia and, of course, the various generic names for fairies and elves that dominate the legends of many Celtic and European lands.

Whilst it is often assumed that these creatures are no more than imaginative stories dreamt up for the purpose of telling cautionary tales and it is also often presumed that the fairy race are said to be tiny creatures but a few inches in height, both of these illusions are false. The stories seem to be worldwide and plumb the darkest depths of our ancient history. The image of a delightful 'Tinkerbell' fluttering on butterfly wings is, in truth, a modern one which owes far more to children's stories than the mythology from which it emerges.

The 'little people', if indeed they did (or do) exist, were said to be about 3 or 4 feet tall and to be so mischievously intrigued by human behaviour that they would often tease and tantalize us with their tricks and devious nature.

Ponder this example. It is not a myth, but supposedly a true story – as true, at least, as any modern claim you will read in the rest of this book. It was first documented in 1937 by Alasdair Alpin MacGregor and so owes nothing to the UFO legends that it so clearly presages. It occurred on the Island of Muck off the coast of Scotland in the year 1912.

Two boys were playing on the beach when they saw a strange boat and were approached by two small beings dressed in green. On board the boat was a small woman with a dog that was to her scale but in our terms about the size of a rat. The beings asked the boys many questions about their lives, talking to them fluently in both English and Gaelic. Then they were given some bread which had the appearance of a walnut and they ate this without question, feeling elated and at peace as they did so. The boys were now enticed to go with the entities who said they had to leave, but the two declined the offer of a trip to fairyland. So they were told instead to remain watching the boat until it reached a certain point far out to sea, and then they would be free to go home. The boys complied and were left with the news that other beings of this strange race would be coming in the future. Shortly afterwards, their sister found the youths with glazed eyes, staring upon an empty sea, lost in a trance.

Almost every feature in this story is a part of UFO lore today. The weird little creatures, their ability to talk the language of whoever they contact, the asking of odd questions, the offering of strange food, the attempt to take away their victim, the strange state of consciousness into which the witnesses lapse and even the bizarre promises of further contact or future visits so glibly made by the intruders.

Can this be mere coincidence? Or does it suggest that alien contact in all its guises has been occurring for a very long time and all that has changed is the way that we choose to interpret what takes place? In Biblical times the creatures were, of course, angelic. In other days they were inevitably viewed as elemental creatures from another sphere of life. Now, today, in this age of spaceships and computers, we, perhaps rather unsurprisingly, regard their boats as UFOs and their origin as a planet round some distant sun.

Who can say which of these multiple interpretations may happen to be the correct one – if indeed any of them are.

In the pages that follow you will find the first comprehensive survey of this alien contact. I intend to draw no conclusions about what it means and imply no truth above any other truth. You are free to evaluate what seems to have been going on. However, I do believe you will find the story fascinating and rather awesome. Think hard on what it indicates *may* be occurring every day and somewhere beneath our noses.

In Part One I will trace the story of this contact throughout the past century, for we have well documented testimony for this period and clear patterns do emerge. I will recount the history in short story fashion reporting what was strange and bizarre. The cases are based upon real claims, the evidence for which you can find intensively discussed and analysed in other books – including many of my own – that were more specifically designed than this one for such a purpose. Roy Sandbach has recreated many of the scenes with his artistic touch so that you can immerse yourself within the unfolding drama and sense the curious nature of this progression of puzzling images.

Part Two of the book will follow this approach through the many alien types met in recent years, giving us a flavour of the entities and their different actions when allegedly in contact with human beings.

For Part Three we move into geographical mode as we look

at how the aliens manifest in various parts of the world. Once again we will find an interesting variety, set within an overall similarity which offers clues towards any meaningful comprehension of what may be going on.

In Part Four we take a brief pause to see what we have discovered so far and draw identikit portraits of the major types of aliens with which humanity appears to have had some sort of rapport throughout the years and literally around the world.

From here we move in Part Five to assess the evidence beyond the anecdotal that to some implies such stories must be real. It is a reasonable tendency of the more cautious minded to suspend judgement and presume such claims are imaginary in nature. That may, of course, be the truth, but hard evidence – such as it is – challenges such a conclusion.

Finally, in Part Six, I will look closely at those cases where the aliens have communicated information to those with whom they have attuned. What do they say? Can it be trusted? Who do they claim to be and where do they allege they come from? What motives do they offer for doing what they do? These questions will be addressed through a series of stories that represent the most confounding of all alien contacts.

At the end of this book we may find ourselves nearer to resolving what lies at the heart of this amazing mystery. I will look at some of the options that are now available to us in seeking a final answer. But on the whole this is not a book that sets out to solve this fascinating riddle. Instead it aims to inform and entertain as well as provide you with an easily digestible but quite extraordinary catalogue of events.

For centuries we have dreamt about contact with another world. What if that contact is already taking place? You are about to find out.

1896: Ships in the Sky

The weird lights first appeared in the skies above California on the night of 17 November 1896. Described as an 'electric arc lamp propelled by some mysterious force' citizens of the state capital, Sacramento, were the first to be amazed by its silent flight. Some even claim they heard singing emerging from the craft as it drifted overhead!

Of course, manned flight by what were to be called airships was then the province of celebrated science-fiction. Jules Verne had published his novel *Robur the Conqueror* about a genius inventor only nine years before this and it was to be almost exactly one year after the California flap, November 1897, when the first metal airship would truly fly into history on a brief jaunt not far from Berlin in Germany.

So the phantom airship wave of late 1896 (which also resurfaced in the mid western states in April 1897 and in Britain in 1909 and 1912) were UFOs in the same sense as today's 'alien spacecraft' are UFOs. They were reports of a fantastic technology dreamt about by writers, under frantic development by aviation experts, but just ahead of what was technically possible for the science of the day.

Who flew the airships? That was the question on everybody's lips and dominating the columns within these frontier newspapers. Many sightings were (correctly) written off as mass hysteria and misperceptions of bright stars and planets such as Venus. But it was not long before hoaxers came forth to claim that they were the mysterious inventor who was secretly flying this technological wonder.

Then the jokers and the bored editors, keen to come up with an even wilder yarn, reported encounters between witnesses and bearded pilots – sometimes Americans, talking about aerial bombing missions to Cuba (with whom the USA then had a dispute), or, occasionally, foreign crewmen speaking some strange language and engaged on nefarious missions. Indeed, in 1912, Winston Churchill became the first politician ever to take UFOs seriously when he warned parliament about the aerial threat from these flying lights which proved to be neither British nor German.

However, according to excellent research by American UFOlogist Jerome Clark, the first claim that these were alien craft – a view that swiftly became rather popular – was reported by Colonel HG Shaw, then engaged in trying to put together an exhibition for a fair in Fresno. It has remarkable comparisons with claims 100 years later.

Shaw and a companion, Camille Spooner, had left the town of Lodi late on the afternoon of 25 November 1896. They were travelling by horse and carriage toward Stockton when their mount reacted in terror and became paralysed. Looking upward the two witnesses observed three human like creatures which were tall and thin with small and very delicate hands. There was a lack of facial and body hair except for a soft downy fur on the skin. The eyes were very large and the mouth and ears small. They looked (and felt) as if they weighed very little and were possessed of a 'strange beauty'.

These entities warbled to one another in a sort of 'monotonous chant'. They had a bag with a nozzle which they put to their mouths from time to time as if taking in gas to help them breathe. They also had an egg-like lamp which glowed very brightly. The terrified Colonel Shaw alleges that they physically attempted to abduct both him and his companion but found their body weight too great and instead turned to flash their light at a nearby bridge. Here, hovering above the water, was a cigar-shaped craft.

The beings returned to their airship in a curious swaying motion in which they almost drifted off the ground. When they reached the machine they sprang into the air and floated into a door in the side of the device, which promptly sailed away. Shaw explained that he was convinced the beings must have come from Mars.

If a tall story, as most people must have assumed when published in late 1896, it was one that was to be very revealing about human imagination. It previewed the type of alien contact that a far more enlightened technological age would take to heart in great abundance. If described in the 1990s rather than the 1890s, very little would have to be changed for this story to be perceived as a very consistent and so perhaps credible claim of attempted alien abduction.

1901: The Aliens Have Landed

Ten year old Frank Warley seems to have been the first person in the twentieth century to claim that he saw alien beings. He reported it to me for what was then the very first time some seventy-seven years after it had happened but added that he remembered it as well as if it were yesterday.

Frank lived in some terraced housing at Bournebrook, near Bournville, in the West Midlands of England. It was a warm summer's afternoon in 1901 and he was taking a short cut along a path behind his back yard when he found a strange object sitting on the grass.

At first he assumed it was a workman's hut because it was small and box-shaped with a turret with a ship's funnel on top and a door in the side. It had a peculiar metal sheen to it and

was a greenish-blue colour. Frank quickly realized this was
something he had never seen before.

Whilst he was puzzling over this structure, about half the size
of a modern small car, the youngster was amazed to find
himself confronted by two beings who stepped from the
doorway into the sunlight. They were small, under 4 feet in
height, and looked very human. Both were clean shaven and
had no noticeably odd features except for their dwarfish size.
They were dressed in tight-fitting one-piece uniforms of a
greenish/grey colour which had a military look about them.

By far the most unusual aspect of the beings was the helmet
that each wore. This was dark, like a cap, and masked the head
and ears completely. But emerging from the top were two
wires, almost like horns on a Viking helmet. These rose about
nine inches into the air and were slightly curved outwards
towards the top. There was no visible way in which this was
attached to the head of the entities.

One of the figures remained in the doorway of the landed
box but the other moved slowly towards Frank. As it did so its
arms became outstretched in a gesture that the boy clearly
recognized as a warning that he must stay back and out of the
way.

Reacting to this silent gesture, Frank had taken a few paces
backwards. As he was doing so the entity was scuttling back
into the box, soon to be joined by its colleague. The door
closed just like a car door (as if on hinges) and within a matter
of seconds the object on the ground sprang into life.

A brilliant flash, recognized later as resembling an electric
arcing effect, lit up the perimeter of the object despite the
bright sunshine. It completed the looping circle around the
object and there was a sudden whooshing noise like a mass of
displaced air and the box shape climbed into the sky in a curved
flight that took it over the rooftops. Frank noted that it carried
a pulsating red light at the rear – something he saw many years
later on aircraft but which in 1901 was unknown.

It seems that there were no marks left on the grass; although
Frank admits that he never thought to search for these. He did
later discover several people in the neighbourhood who
claimed that they either heard the whooshing noise or saw the
blinking light in the sky.

What is most intriguing may be that Frank never used the
word UFO in his description of this object. He merely called it

a 'funny vehicle'. He says that at the time when it took place there were no UFOs and he was already 'well advanced in age' before there were. By the time he first heard the term he had long accepted what he saw.

Many were the times that Frank attempted to write off his experience as a boyish dream. But he explains that in his youth there were often illustrations in newspapers and magazines depicting 'transport of the future' and these invariably showed airships or floating craft with clumsy propellers. None depicted anything remotely like the calm, quiet and efficient little object that he saw. If a dream, then why would he not conjure up something he was familiar with? And if a dream how could he reliably foresee the type of UFO that would feature in alien contact stories many years into the future?

1926: A Meeting With Three Wise Men

Just imagine the sheer terror that an encounter with strange creatures can bring, especially in an age when there was nothing to compare it with. This was certainly true for youngster Henry Thomas who reported to UFO researcher Peter Hough many years later how a childish prank in the roaring twenties rapidly turned into a nightmare.

Thomas was upset at having been put to bed early on a dark November evening. His friends were all outside roaming the terraced streets of the industrial town of Bolton, Lancashire, which was then gripped by both the oncoming winter and the paralysing miners' strike which had nearly brought the country to its knees.

Deciding that he would risk retribution from his police officer father, Henry scuttled out of the bedroom and out into the night, his parents too engrossed in a radio programme to be alert to his less than stealthy departure.

Meeting his friends, the gang set out to play a game of hide and seek, which involved Henry searching the soldierly rows of brick-walled back yards with their rickety outside toilets and grimy facades. But instead of finding his mates, Henry found something that was much worse than he had bargained for.

One back gate was mysteriously ajar. Wondering if his friends had left it this way in error as they hastened into the yard, Henry dared to peek within. His friends were not there. But the most frightening sight he would ever face in his life was waiting for him.

Looking into the house back window were three beings. They were of normal adult height; although one was perhaps 6 feet tall. But he knew right away that they were not ordinary men because they were dressed in the strangest clothes he had ever witnessed, suits made up of rolls of tubing or rubber which resembled the 'Michelin Tyre' man advertisements he would later see so often. The clothing was silver grey and their thick boots were black. Yet each had a transparent dome-like helmet from which emerged tubes that connected into a breathing tank fastened to their backs.

Henry Thomas stared in awe. In doing so he must have somehow attracted the attention of these beings as they swivelled around to confront him. Then he saw their faces and panic filled his gut.

The heads were pale and shaped like lightbulbs, with eyes that were dark and slit-like, having no obvious mouth and a vertical line in place of a nose. They reminded him most of an owl, wise and animalistic yet somehow inducing great fear. From one emerged a strange gurgling, mumbling sound and suddenly all three turned in his direction and began to move towards him. At once Henry fled the scene and ran all the way home.

Rushing through the door he blurted out the story right away. He was scolded for his unauthorised expedition but his parents seemed to know that this was no joke. For the reality of his close encounter was etched upon his blood-drained face.

Of course, this was never interpreted as a meeting with aliens. These were the product of only a few Penny Dreadfuls at the time and the term UFO was still decades away from being invented. 'The three wise men' was how the family came to refer to this early close encounter. But it is remarkably like several similar episodes during the first half of this century; an inexplicable meeting with the unknown.

We might speculate if the boy had seen rat catchers or fumigators and misinterpreted their strange garb for something more mysterious. But the description of those faces and even the Michelin Man suits became a not uncommon feature amidst the UFO waves of years to come. Henry was to be joined by thousands of other people who saw beings with heads shaped like lamps and powerfully disturbing eyes. Perhaps he was simply one of the first to interrupt their puzzling mission.

1947: Take Your Pick

In June 1947 the phrase 'flying saucer' was first invented after sightings of strange lights in the north-western United States. It took only a few weeks for the arrival of true close encounters of the third kind – as meetings with alien beings were to be termed.

The location of the earliest intriguing one was extremely remote – the Alps north of Venice, Italy, on the border with Austria. The victim in this harrowing encounter was an artist, writer and geologist by the name of Professor Rapuzzi Johannis, who was following his passion for the rocks by trekking up a valley on the side of the mountain known as Carnico del Col Gentile near the town of Villa Santina.

It was a bright fresh morning around 9 a.m. on 14 August 1947 and Johannis was alone several thousand feet up the hillside edging his way upwards through layers of gypsum beside a dry river bed. Suddenly he observed a red object on the ground and, donning his spectacles, realized that it was a lens-shaped object some 30 feet wide and made of polished metal. It seemed to be partially imbedded in the rock of the hill slope.

The UFO stories had not reached Italy from the USA and so he looked at this in great puzzlement. Was it a secret Russian plane, he asked himself? Glancing around in the rather forlorn hope that someone else might be on the mountainside to support his story he saw two boys at the edge of a wooded area from which he had just emerged. So he shouted at them to come and take a look. Then he began to walk towards them both, stopping in horror when he realized that these were not boys at all but two strange beings only just over 3 feet tall.

As he stared at these creatures the geologist reports that he felt drained of all energy and a curious lightheadedness or dream-like quality filled the surroundings. This peculiar aura to close encounters is now a very well known feature and is called the Oz Factor. It suggests that witnesses are plunged into an altered state of consciousness at the onset of the experience.

The two little men had now moved slowly towards Johannis. They wore close-fitting blue garments that seemed translucent and the oddest part of their appearance were their heads, which were larger than the proportions of their bodies should dictate. There was no sign of hair, but they did wear tight-fitting dark skull caps. The mouth was a slit that opened and shut like a fish's gills and the nose was long and straight. However, it was the eyes that really stood out. They were huge, round and plum-coloured without any trace of eyebrows or lashes.

At closer approach the scientist could see that the beings had a faint and odd greenish cast to their skins (this possibly being the origin of the much abused phrase in UFO lore, 'little green men'). Their hands were also more like claws.

After staring at one another for some moments the professor raised his long geologist's pick in a gesture intended as a friendly wave, shouting at the same time 'who are you?'. Perhaps interpreting these moves as a hostile act, one entity rapidly raised a hand from his side to touch a belt that was around his midriff. A flash or puff of light shot from this and hit Johannis in the arm.

The scientist was immediately knocked senseless by this attack, thrown to the ground and dazed. At the same time his long-handled pick was snatched from his hand as if grabbed by a crane and flew through the air on its own to crash to the ground 6 feet away.

Johannis now felt as if he had been struck by an electric charge and could only painfully prop himself on one arm as the beings came over and took up the pick. They were so close he could see their lightly-boned chests quivering like a dog when it pants for breath. Then the beings returned to the lens-shaped object and vanished, presumably inside it somehow. Moments later it shot from the rocks, sending a cascade of loose stones down into the river bed.

The terrified witness lay helpless on the ground, afraid that the hovering device might somehow crush him. But after a minute or two it inexplicably shrunk in size and silently 'imploded' or simply disappeared. With this a tremendous blast of air hit him, rolling him down the slopes and sending him smashing into the river bed. It was several hours before he had the energy to get up and hobble to the village of Raveo where he told the innkeeper he had merely fallen off a rock face.

1952: The Man from Venus

In the late 1940s and early 1950s a few more alien encounters took place but many UFO researchers rejected them as simply too fantastic. They rarely made headlines or filled popular books as reports of flying saucers were already beginning to do. It was as if these claims of 'UFO pilots' were just too much to take in all at once.

However, this was not to be the case when a whole new set of adventure stories hit the presses in 1952. The contactee movement was to become an instant global attraction with its main protagonists hailed as celebrities, packing lecture halls and selling hundreds of thousands of copies of their optimistic books.

In fact, contactee stories could not be more different from the first few 'normal' alien contacts such as that of Rapuzzi Johannis. There was no fear or total alienness to the encounter. Instead, these tales were like something from a *Boys Own* comic book – akin to a Biggles episode – the sort of popular fodder then filling radio networks as the earth edged slowly towards the dawn of the space age.

The overriding difference with the contactee cases was that the witness was not a victim of circumstance chancing upon strange creatures doing their own thing. Instead the contactee himself (it was usually a man) was the focus of the story, in some cases saving the solar system from catastrophe and chosen as special by the benevolent spacemen.

The first of what became hundreds of contactees (some still thriving today, especially amidst the new age movement of the American west) was George Adamski. A Polish emigree in 1893, Adamski was a moderately successful presenter of occultist tales on local California radio and author of fairly primitive science-fiction. He dreamed of space as he worked his food and drink stand on the slopes of Mount Palomar, home of a big astronomical observatory. Using a telescope of his own, which often made people think he was a professional astronomer, he took pictures of what he claimed were alien spacecraft and first wrote of these in *Fate* magazine in 1950. But far stranger things were to follow.

On 20 November 1952, Adamski and some friends drove into the California desert with, he told them, the intention of seeing a spaceship. Sure enough, some said they did see one, but Adamski convinced them it had come for him. They waited a mile away as he went into the desert to have what he claimed was a contact with a man from Venus.

The human-like being had long blond hair and corresponded with the witness through sign language and telepathy. Adamski learned how there were 'mother ships' in orbit and smaller 'scout ships' with which they visited earth. The Venusians were a very friendly race who were afraid of human aggression and our abuse of terrible weapons such as atom bombs. The being took from his camera Adamski's undeveloped close-up shots of the landed scout ship (the alien himself was camera shy!) and some days later in a second encounter flew by and handed the contactee his film back. His evidence of the spaceship had been replaced with an image of a set of symbols which nobody has ever decoded.

Adamski's account of his contact was picked up by Irish writer Desmond Leslie and added at the last minute to his otherwise mundane book about UFO sightings. The enterprising publisher saw the potential, making Adamski's tale the focus of the book which appeared in 1953 as *Flying Saucers Have Landed* and was an instant bestseller.

Over the next few years more ghost written books 'by' Adamski appeared in which ever more sensational claims followed. He met aliens from most planets in our solar system (with silly names like Firkon which were apparently invented for effect by his uncredited ghost writer Charlotte Blodget). He also took more photographs of flying saucers, often through his telescope, and told of visits to see trees and rivers on the moon and the esoteric teachings of the kindly spacefolk, which usually rather notably comprised not dissimilar thoughts to those Adamski had expressed himself in days before his alleged close encounters.

Eventually he toured Europe where the Queen of Holland asked to meet him and in 1963 he even claimed he had met the Pope (the Vatican deny this). He died in April 1965, his views having split the UFO community into two camps which still exist today. The occult-orientated UFOlogists or fervent believers in friendly extraterrestrials accept much of what Adamski said as gospel, literally. Most UFO researchers, however, believe his stories were at best hallucinations and perhaps outright fantasies.

There is no doubt that Adamski's evidence is barely persuasive. His photographs have convinced few and many allege analysis shows them to be small, crude fakes. His stories about conditions on other planets in the solar system were found to be scientifically absurd even before he died.

Of the other celebrated contactees that followed Adamski,

most told similar tales; although the aliens were often different in appearance, came from other places (including invisible planets behind the sun or in parallel universes) and had equally corny names (eg., Aura Rhanes). Their philosophies almost always told of peace, love and anti-nuclear messages but rarely matched one another in detail.

The contactee movement rapidly became a sub-culture in its own right with colourful conventions and magazines, some of which survive today. The Aetherius Society, for example, founded in 1954 by London taxi driver George King, when told of his election as earth's representative to a sort of interplanetary parliament, remains a strong focus of bene-volent alien philosophy with a significant often erudite membership base, especially in Britain and California. They deny they are a contactee cult.

There are some who seriously speculate that a few of the early contactees (none ever being named specifically but *not* including the Aetherians) might have somehow been duped by the intelligence services, who set up their contacts. What sounds like the most absurd form of paranoia has an element of support from documents released under the American 'Freedom of Information' Act.

Around the time when the first contactees flourished, January 1953, the CIA convened a then top secret meeting in Washington, inviting key scientists to consider how to defuse all serious public interest in UFOs. They talked about employing cartoonists like Walt Disney to make trivial films and turn UFO sightings into a joke. From the released files it seems that in that strange age of Communist witch hunts the CIA believed an enemy power might simulate a phoney UFO wave, creating mass hysteria and clogging the arteries of communication across America!

In an assessment of the policies eventually adopted (which comprised various tricks to try to obscure the unexplained UFO evidence) the CIA refer to how the contactee literature had reduced the credibility of UFO evidence in the eyes of many people. Of their (still partly secret) tactics employed to aid their task they note darkly that these were 'achieving well' the things that they had been set up to do.

1954: The Alien Invasion of Europe

Whatever the tactics of the American intelligence agencies, the debatable motives of any of the contactees or the rather surprising indifference of the flourishing UFO investigation movement to their tales, the aliens were not about to be forced into oblivion.

By 1954 science-fiction movies were beginning to speculate wildly about alien contact, with all sorts of monsters landing on earth in stylised flying saucers, taking over people's bodies, oozing gelatinous slime and generally being about as obnoxious and unfriendly as one could imagine. These popular movies were the exact opposite of the contactee philosophies of friendly, human-like space brothers who always had our best interests at heart. But equally, they were a million light years away from the truth of those very simple alien contact 'realities' that had been quietly accumulating up until that time.

Would the Hollywood 'B' movies such as *The Thing From Another World* (1951), *It Came From Outer Space* and *Invaders From Mars* (both 1953) affect the 'true' alien contact cases? Whilst a tiny few monster sightings did occur, most notably the Hopkinsville, Kentucky, case from August 1955, when a family shot at a small goblin-like creature with huge pointed ears that trapped them in their house, these were remarkable mostly by their absence in the face of the movie-image bombardment.

Whilst it was not recognized at the time, either by the media or by the UFO experts, the relatively few alien contacts that were occurring were strongly following the same lines as those which had dominated the subject since the very start. But what did change was that in October 1954 they suddenly exploded in numbers.

We were by then used to having waves of UFO sightings occurring around the world, notably the USA, and focused into a few days or weeks. What we had never had before was a spate of seemingly credible alien contact stories. Until autumn that year when one struck Europe. It defied the then still secret CIA initiative and made some UFO experts at last sit up and take notice of these claims about seeing the UFO-nauts.

Soon after this wave had begun, a typically impressive case occurred at the village of Quarouble, near Valenciennes, on the extreme north-eastern border of France with Belgium. The witness was a thirty-four year old steel mill worker who lived

with his wife and young children astride a freight railway line
which had a local crossing point.

The witness, Marius Dewilde, was reading late one evening
when his dog began to bark. As this was an isolated spot he
feared a prowler and went outside with a flashlight to confront
the intruders.

Once outside he immediately saw a dark mass on the tracks
which he assumed to be a wagon or cart of some sort. But these
thoughts were swiftly distracted by his dog, which came
crawling on its stomach, whining and yelping, in evident, but
thankfully temporary, distress. The sound of footsteps were
heard scuttling away and Dewilde pointed his torch in their
direction. He was not prepared for what the beam was to
illuminate.

Shuffling slowly towads the 'wagon' on the railway line were
two beings dressed in dark-coloured divers' suits. The head part
was particularly big in comparison with the body and they were
only about 3½ feet tall altogether. Without thinking he gave
pursuit but had only gone a few steps when a brilliant flash (like
a magnesium flare) shot from the dark shape on the tracks and
struck him. Immediately the man was frozen still, paralysed
and incapable of even crying out.

The beam remained fixed on Dewilde for some moments,
during which he heard the footsteps retreat. Then suddenly the
beam extinguished and he was instantly released from its grip.
He ran towards the spot on the tracks but was only in time to
see the dark shape rising into the air with steam coming from its
underside whilst an odd whistling noise was emitted. The shape
moved away and then turned into a red glow which sped out of
sight. Several local country folk later came forward to report
seeing this glow.

Dewilde went to the local police immediately after telling his
wife and neighbour, but he was still in a state of shock and
disorientation and making little sense. Unhappy with their
response he went to see the police commissioner, who was
convinced and called in a special military unit. They found
stones by the track that had been made brittle by great heat and
five indentations on the sleepers which, engineers told them,
indicated an object weighing 30 tons had pressed down from
above.

For the first time an alien contact offered hard, physical
evidence for its reality. But the French government team who

took the samples away for analysis clammed up. The local police later complained that they could not get answers as to what the experts discovered.

A few weeks later it seems that Dewilde had a second encounter with the aliens but he was so disgusted at the way in which he was treated by officialdom after the first experience that he said merely that he would keep the details to himself. It is possible that this second episode was very important as it was soon to become a common theme for witnesses to receive return visitations. The alien contact moved on a phase from simply stopping people in their tracks (as with Johannis and Dewilde) and began actively communicating with them.

The little men with large heads put in many reappearances over the next few weeks, particularly in France. Aggression such as at Quarouble was not uncommon. For instance, on 16 October, at Baillolet, south of Dieppe, a doctor in his car was struck by a beam which created an electric shock sensation and cut out both the engine and lights. This was one of the very first so-called 'car stop' cases which became a favourite mode of initiating alien contact. Indeed, even today, one of the most dangerous places to be if you fear possible alien contact is in a car on a lonely road late at night.

At Baillolet, the doctor was paralysed and unconscious for an unknown time, or at least he recalls nothing more until the UFO and entity were disappearing and his car engine and lights began to work again.

It is possible that cases such as this one, and several others from the 1954 wave, might hide deeper memories which neither investigator nor witnesses suspected and so were never sought. The possibility that at times the alien contact may have gone further was to be revealed as the next step was taken in this strange sequence of events.

1957: An Encounter of the Closest Kind

UFO experts were struggling to come to terms with stories of little aggressive beings who apparently preferred not to be disturbed doing whatever it was that they were evidently doing. How did such claims relate to the taller, rather blond and more human-looking 'space brothers' that the contactees were reporting?

It was hard enough for the private UFO groups now

springing up in abundance to establish the reality of UFOs in the face of a new policy by the US Air Force (as well as, although the UFOlogists did not then know it, the CIA). This was to convince the public at all costs that every UFO sighting was simply a misperception of a mundane object, such as an aircraft or weather balloon. Since serious researchers knew that this diagnosis was true in many cases their task was even harder.

As such, the alien stories were still handled with considerable reservation. However, the European wave had impressed upon French UFOlogists such as one of the best UFO writers of the 1950s (Aime Michel) and a young computer expert and science-fiction writer about to move to the USA (Jacques Vallee) that there was extraordinary consistency between them which was hard to dismiss out of hand.

Nevertheless, this inbred reluctance to ask the public to believe too much was a factor in why the most extraordinary alien contact of them all was sat upon by the investigators for several years, sharing it only with a few other UFOlogists. The hope was that something else like it would eventually occur and they could then produce this fantastic story as support. At least they could genuinely argue that it had not been the stimulus for future copycat hoaxes, a favourite theory of the sceptics when faced with the obvious patterns that were emerging.

This closest of all encounters came from South America, where cases just like those in Europe and North America had been going on. But they were difficult to separate out from a vociferous tabloid media that had a fondness for colourful tales.

In fact, during November and December 1954, immediately in the wake of the European wave, the little men focused their attention on Brazil, Argentina and Venezuela (although often here described as extremely hirsute – a unique feature about South American cases, especially in the earlier years). Otherwise the stories were identical, with witnesses being rendered senseless by beams of light from a hand-held weapon or fired directly from the UFO and paralysed for long enough to enable the creatures to effect their getaway.

Between April and October 1957 the world was set to launch the first object into earth orbit (the Soviet sputnik). In that time the press, especially in Brazil, reported several claims of on-board encounters which seemed to form a bridge between the contactee stories of the past few years and the aggressive alien contacts. Typically a witness might have been a respected member of the community (eg., a doctor) who had seen an object land and felt an urge to go inside where he then communicated by telepathy with what were usually the blonder and more gentle beings of contactee lore, if often smaller than average height. A typical message was offered about the wicked ways of the world, but there was no desire to form a movement as with the contactee and no long-term communications. It was a curiously hybrid experience.

In November 1957 a well-known Brazilian journalist (Joao Martins) who had already written several articles about UFOs, received two letters from a farmer in a poor rural area. These described his fantastic story. Martins contacted a Rio de Janeiro doctor called Olavo Fontes and they decided the case warranted study. They sent twenty-three year old Antonio Villas Boas the fare to travel several hundred miles from his home at Sao Francisco de Sales and come to Dr Fontes' surgery.

Whilst that might seem like a motive for a hoax, it is worth noting that Boas lost considerable money that he would have received from his work on the family farm in making the journey to attend what was at best a non profit-making research exercise. This spanned several days in February 1958, after which Martins and Fontes chose to keep the story to themselves and the farmer, though disappointed, never argued. Again Villas Boas made no attempt to sell his story to the press as he was told he could do and must have been a temptation given his meagre resources. That should be recalled when judging the sincerity of this amazing encounter.

Boas took turns in cultivating the fields with his brothers and worked the nightshift, manning the tractor. A few days earlier he had seen a light in the fields and on 14 October 1957 he saw it again with his older brother. It was sufficiently brilliant to hurt the eyes.

The next night, around 1 a.m. on 15/16 October, Villas Boas was alone in the fields driving his tractor when a red 'star' appeared and swooped at him, descending over the machine and pouring out so much light that it swamped the tractor headlights. He was terrified, but unable to know what to do. The tractor speed could not outrun this thing and the soil was so soft and churned up that to try to run through it in the pitch dark would be very dangerous. He saw that the red light was a spotbeam at the front of a rounded object with a rotating cupola on top. When it moved to the side and ejected three legs, evidently ready to land only yards away, the farmer decided he had no other choice. He put the tractor into gear and slowly chugged away. He had gone only a few feet when the engine and lights of his machine died simultaneously and, despite frantic efforts, he could not get them to function again.

Opening his tractor door, Boas jumped to the damp earth but had only made a few steps when he was grabbed from the side by a human-like being about 5 feet tall. Reacting instinctively he pushed the being away and it fell to the ground. But the farmer's escape was soon aborted by three other beings, of more normal height, who grabbed him and lifted him off the ground, dragging him towards their machine, looking curiously at him every time he cried out and screamed at them. They were all covered in grey one-piece overalls and large helmets, hiding all but the eyes.

At the UFO they unravelled a metal ladder and took him up into a small, square room. The farmer noted how the inside was as bright as day and when the doors closed how these blended seamlessly into the wall so you could not tell where they were. He was then taken (via another vanishing door) into a second room which was semi-circular in shape with just a few backless chairs and a table or bed fashioned out of white shiny metal, 'welded' into the floor by a single column or support. The beings spoke to each other in monosyllabic yelps, two of them holding Boas in place all the time. They seemed to set upon a course of action and others appeared, stripping the farmer naked and leaving him in an atmosphere that he noted was cold like a fridge.

The beings then proceeded to cover the entirety of Antonio's body with a watery liquid that was thick and felt like gel of some sort. It quickly evaporated or was absorbed by the skin. He was then forcefully led into another room with the walls studded by square lights and a strange 'bed'. It had a pronounced hump in the middle which made it uncomfortable to lie or sit upon. Two men took samples of blood from him, sucking these up into siphon-like tubes. At the time he felt no pain but his skin burned a little afterwards. After this they all left him alone in the room for what he believes was as long as half an hour.

Eventually he began to smell a noxious odour which seemed to be coming from a gas escaping into the room through the walls. He ran to the corner of the room and was violently sick, then felt better and went to sit on the bed, nearly exhausted.

Another long period passed and he heard sounds and turned to see something he had not expected. It was a woman, human-like in all senses except that her face was somewhat angular and she was only 4½ to 5 feet tall. Her eyes were cat-like but beautiful and her hair long and white. However, elsewhere she had blood red body hair (eg., under her armpits) that was soft and downy.

Villas Boas sheepishly reported that he could not explain why he became sexually aroused, but did so. As a result he was readily seduced; although at no time did the woman kiss him (she nipped him with her mouth a few times and made barking noises!). When intercourse was completed she quickly removed herself, as if glad it was over, then looked at the terrified man almost with pity. She smiled, rubbed her belly, pointed at him and then into the air. He interpreted this, a bit oddly, as a warning that she would come back and take him away with her, but a more obvious possibility is that she was saying 'the purpose of this is that I have your child up there in space'.

The woman left and was not seen again, but in the meantime Villas Boas was taken back to the first room with the table and swivel chairs and left for some time as the uniformed men conversed with each other. At one point he tried to take an object a bit like a clock from the room but was stopped angrily. Then he was taken out and given a walking tour of the ship from the cupola rim surrounded its exterior. Finally the being acting as guide gestured he return down the ladder and step back.

Moments later the cupola began to rotate faster and faster, there was a noise like displaced air and the object rose upward. It then glowed very brightly and shot off like a bullet sideways across the sky. The farmer found that his tractor still would not work and upon arrival back at the farmhouse discovered that about four hours had passed whilst he was apparently inside the object.

Over the next couple of weeks Villas Boas suffered physical symptoms of weakness, tiredness and nausea, coupled with the anticipated nightmares and insomnia and also several small bleeding lesions and bruises with no obvious cause that appeared on his body. Dr Fontes noted that these were consistent with mild radiation sickness.

Although they chose not to publish the story their original report adds that they found the farmer, who had only a very basic education (nothing beyond primary school level), to be rational and unimaginative. He did not offer the details of the sexual liaison either freely or with relish. Indeed, he exhibited deep embarrassment whenever the topic was discussed, feeling ashamed of how easily he had submitted.

Five years later (in 1962) details of the story were sent to British UFO journal, *Flying Saucer Review*, but they were not translated and written up for an English-speaking audience until late 1964. They did not appear in Brazil until some time after that.

In the meantime something was to happen elsewhere which was to change the whole significance of this incredible story.

1961: Into the Spider's Web

Four years after the Villas Boas case had taken place, but when very few UFOlogists and only those in South America knew about it, on the Canadian/American border a few thousand miles to the north – a new case was set to erupt which would have momentous repercussions.

It was late on the night of 19 September 1961. Betty Hill, a forty-one year old child welfare worker, and her thirty-nine year old Ethiopian descended husband, Barney, who worked for the post office, were returning from a holiday in southern Canada towards their New Hampshire home. They were engaged on the long drive through the White Mountains which had only very limited traffic and isolated communities back in those days.

They were puzzled for some time by a white light which seemed to follow the car and even stopped several times to discuss it. Controversy rages about its origin, with sceptics insisting it has to be the planet Jupiter or Saturn (or even the moon) which were all in that part of the sky. However, the Hills say it moved even when they stopped and the ever sceptical Barney speculated about both aircraft and satellites.

Eventually, at a place called Indian Head, they stopped again and this time Barney got out, 'feeling an urge' to walk towards the object, as if lured to it like a fly into a spider's web.

Through binoculars he said he saw what Betty confirmed was now a banana or pancake-like object (he also saw windows in the front and via binoculars 'people' standing behind them). Barney was oblivious to the cries from his wife calling him to return to the car. Suddenly, realizing that he might be in danger, he did go back and they drove away. But then there was a curious bleeping sound inside and they both felt very drowsy. The next thing they recall is a second bleep or bump and everything was now back to normal, but there was no clear memory of what had happened in between.

They found themselves a few miles south of the place where Barney had got out, not a distance that would have taken two hours to cover. Yet, some weeks later, a puzzling excessive duration for the journey came out in conversation when they went over the details with UFOlogists.

Upon arrival home around 5.30 a.m. the Hills noticed some odd spots on the metal body of the car. A compass held up to it (suggested by Betty's sister who had seen a UFO) had swung wildly around. This was enough to cause concern and they reported the matter to Pease Air Force base and to a UFO group called NICAP whose name Betty found in the library.

That original letter still exists on file in Chicago at the J Allen Hynek Center for UFO Studies (I have seen it). Via the American Freedom of Information Act the statement recorded by Pease Air Force Base thirty-six hours after the sighting is also on record. According to Jacques Vallee this indicates that at 2.14 a.m. (slap bang in the middle of the self diagnosed missing two hours of the journey) 'a strange incident' had occurred at the base. Vallee says this was a radar tracking of an unknown object. If so it is vital corroboration for this case.

On 21 October 1961 astronomer and UFO researcher Walter Webb came to interview the Hills at NICAP's request and set in motion what was to become one of the most talked about UFO cases in history, eventually made into a very responsible 1975 TV movie entitled *the UFO Incident*. Webb wrote a fair account of the story and was impressed by the witnesses, despite his then admitted scepticism of alien contacts. Even four weeks after the sighting when he first met the Hills, Betty had become knowledgeable through her avid reading. She went on to investigate cases and become a part of the UFO community for almost thirty years, particularly after her husband tragically died of a cerebral hemorrhage in 1969.

Ten days after the experience, Betty Hill had a series of dreams in which the couple had been abducted into the craft and physically examined by beings who showed her a map of space. These traumatic nightmares ended after a few days but she shared them with Barney.

Both witnesses were bothered by the question of missing time and lack of memories for this period, but with Barney the anxiety became physically acute. In spring 1962 they consulted a doctor and, after going the rounds of several specialists, they finally reached Boston psychiatrist Dr Benjamin Simon, a respected ex-Harvard practitioner in memory retrieval and stress relief. He began treatment in January 1964.

Six months of hypnosis sessions followed, involving Barney at first but then both witnesses. Dr Simon stressed that he was not investigating their UFO story and had no opinion one way or another about its reality.

However, the psychiatrist did speculate about a possible condition whereby Barney's anxiety might have resulted from his unconscious absorption of Betty's dreams shortly after the car journey. But in 1966 he told journalist John Fuller (who was first to document the case in his excellent book *The Interrupted Journey*) that he did not think the couple were psychotic, hallucinating or lying. Dr Simon also confirmed that they paid substantial sums to partly fund his treatment, which suggested their sincerity to him. But, according to UFO sceptic Philip Klass he later said that he did not think there was a 'real' abduction. He felt the added 'memories' were imagination.

During many hours of taped hypnosis 'memories', the Hills relived their traumatic car journey and a revised story emerged.

Barney strongly resisted Betty's interpretation of the light as being something strange. In an early session he is heard arguing as he relives the moment in the car; 'Betty! This is *not* a flying saucer. What are you doing this for? You want to believe in this thing ... I don't.'

But once the barrier is overcome Barney Hill talked of getting out of the car and feeling like a rabbit caught in a spotlight. The beings in the craft were seen clearly and he focused particularly on their eyes, which he kept repeating looked Chinese or like the Cheshire cat in *Alice in Wonderland* (ie., slanted or cat-like, as in the Villas Boas case). He also heard a voice in his mind telling him not to be afraid.

Barney ran back to the car and they drove off to the point

where the beeping sounds were heard and figures stood in the road. Betty described how the car was vibrating as if full of electricity (identical to that obscure report from a French doctor in 1954 – see page 23).

She seemed to have a fairly normal conversation with one of the beings (who had a foreign accent; although later she noted that telepathy might have been involved). He used colloquialisms freely such as 'Oh, so ...' and 'back in no time'. This forms such a part of Betty's testimony that both sceptic Klass and UFOlogist John Spencer argue that aliens ought not to be so precise with our language, especially when later Betty claims they respond oddly to her words. In fact, they asked many questions like 'What is a year?' which suggested that they had a very poor grasp of linguistic skills. Or was it that, if Betty was conversing telepathically, this was her interpretation of what they were saying using language stored in her own mind?

Barney reports that he felt a floating sensation and semi-consciousness until inside a room on a table or bed where a suction-like device was placed over his groin area and something painlessly extracted. This is another detailed comparison with the Villas Boas case. But in February 1964 when he spoke these words, that case was unknown.   Betty says she saw her husband being dragged aboard by a couple of the beings but they persuaded her not to resist by advising that they would let them both go unharmed and only wanted to 'do some tests.'

Once up a ramp and inside a room the couple were separated. Betty describes how she had hair, nail and other samples extracted and how a large eye-like device was scanned over her body. Then a huge needle, bigger than anything she had ever seen before, was placed into her navel. She cried out in pain and one being waved a hand in front of her eyes and the pain simply disappeared. They told her this was a pregnancy test, which she disputed. Ten years later, as the first steps towards the eventual 'test tube baby' revolution began, a remarkably similar process was developed to extract eggs via a long needle-like tube placed into the navel. Some researchers see this as an important vindication for the case; although whether we should expect alien doctors to duplicate our own future technology in such exact detail is more open to doubt.

The aliens seen by the couple also had similarities with the Villas Boas case; notably the small size (not much over 5 feet tall). Betty reported that one being who was in charge (she called him the 'leader') seemed different to the others. Barney appears not to have seen this entity and his description is slightly different to Betty's (notably concerning the nose and mouth). However, both report that the face had an elongated chin and skin was an unusual waxy grey or almost white colour.

The beings also had considerable curiosity. Betty reports they were intrigued because Barney had false teeth and hers would not come out (they tried!). They kept her waiting in another room whilst they did more tests on her husband, seemingly puzzled by his difference in colour.

Just as happened to Villas Boas, after the physicals were over, Betty got a bit of a tour of the UFO and was shown a 'star map' which they explained depicted 'trading routes'. She asked them to show their home star but they explained that if she did not know where earth was, such an exercise was futile. This had, of course, been part of her earlier 'dream'.

Later, an amateur astronomer, Marjorie Fish, suggested a possible interpretation of the map which Betty redrew under hypnosis. Taking a few liberties (sceptics say too many) it suggested that the 'home world' of the beings might revolve around one of the stars of Zeta Reticulii.

Hypnosis is a very difficult issue to evaluate in connection with the retrieval of missing memories. Dr Simon made one thing clear from the outset and his caution has been echoed by dozens of doctors who have carried out similar 'time loss' experiments in UFO cases since 1964. Whilst the state of consciousness that is induced by hypnosis can facilitate better recall it can also trigger creativity and even fantasy. For this reason it is rarely used in courts of law to help witnesses remember crimes that they may have observed. It can be a real problem distinguishing truth from fiction in a 'normal' situation like a bank robbery. Imagine the difficulties when the memories are so out of this world that there is not even a 'norm' to judge them against.

By the time the hypnosis began Betty was clearly very well steeped in UFO literature and had already discussed her recurring dreams of an onboard abduction with others, notably her husband. So any analysis of the later hypnosis storyline must be somewhat compromised.

On the other hand, ample documentation exists to prove how the slow unraveling of the Hills' story predated any possible awareness of the Villas Boas case which it obviously complements extraordinarily well. Similarly, when the Hills' story leaked to journalists in October 1965 (nobody is quite sure how) and was eventually written up in great detail in Fuller's book in 1966, the Villas Boas case had now been fully documented via Britain's *Flying Saucer Review* but was not known to the general public, or even to many UFOlogists.

In other words, these two intertwined cases are as near as we can get to being independent of one another. This was a situation that could never be repeated. By 1967 Fuller's book was being serialised all over the English-speaking world and the story of what a UFO abduction was like became almost instantly known to millions of people. No longer could we ignore the fact that nearly all future witnesses probably must have come across the subject at some point in their lives, even if they had consciously forgotten about the details. This made cases explored under hypnosis particularly vulnerable to other, less exotic, interpretations.

1964: The Case that Convinced the World

By 1964 UFOs were in something of a recession. People had in a sense become rather bored by the endless stream of reports and all too predictable official denials. There were fewer sightings being reported, the media had lost a lot of interest and most people's eyes were turned towards space in a more literal sense as the Soviets and the Americans battled to be the first to leave earth orbit and land a manned vehicle on the moon.

So far as alien contact was concerned, the cases remained low key and sporadic in occurrence. Although both the Villas Boas and Hill abduction stories had by now happened, neither were public knowledge and not even UFOlogy had attempted to incorporate them into its philosophy as yet. It is fair to say that amongst serious researchers, lights in the sky and disc-like craft were readily accepted but claims of seeing aliens remained tainted by the aftertaste of the contactee movement.

But then a sighting occurred which was to raise the profile of this type of a case to a quite unprecedented level. It made believers out of former sceptics.

Dr J Allen Hynek, for example, was an astronomer who for seventeen years had been chief science consultant to the ongoing US government enquiry. He was facing peer ridicule for this brave act but also UFOlogists' wrath for being part of a perceived cover-up and acting too cautious by half when it came to how many sightings he was prepared to explain away.

The US air force called him in to investigate this dramatic 1964 landing. But far from tow the party line and preach simple solutions he was to go on record as calling this one of the most important cases in UFO history. In his memoirs of this period published in 1977 after all government enquiry had ended he wrote of the events: 'Despite my strong desire to find a natural explanation for the sighting (I was still unconvinced about the reality of [alien contacts], I could find none ... It is my opinion that a *real, physical* event occurred.'

At 5.45 p.m. on 24 April 1964 an experienced thirty year old police officer, Lonnie Zamora, from the desert town of Socorro, New Mexico, was on patrol in pursuit of a speeding car. He chased it out of town but was then distracted by a roaring noise and saw orange and blue-coloured flames in the sky, low on the horizon. Knowing that a hut with dynamite stores was in that area he feared an explosion and, giving this priority, broke off the chase and drove into the hilly scrubland.

He had to make three attempts to get the patrol car up a steep incline, but he had a better view of the tapering flame which seemed to be descending into an open piece of canyon. The roaring noise lowered in pitch and then stopped, as did the flames. At the top of the slope he saw an egg-like craft, which he at first assumed was a car overturned by vandals. He had sun shades on top of spectacles and in the low sunlight found it difficult to be sure from inside the moving car.

As he edged the car as close as he could towards the object, then paused for a few moments, Zamora saw two 'kids' beside the polished white metal, reinforcing his theory about vandals. They seemed to wear white one-piece suits and be slightly smaller than most adult males (or exactly the size in both the Hill and Villas cases). One of the 'kids' turned to look at him as if surprised to be interrupted.

Now convinced of what he was seeing, Zamora took his eyes from them and edged the car forward, calling on the radio to base that he was investigating a 'possible 10-40' (the code for an accident). Meanwhile he pulled to a halt, still talking on the radio, and got out, dropping the mike as he did so. He bent down to pick up the mike and was hit by a loud roar which escalated in pitch and was not unlike a jet engine. Glancing into the canyon he saw flames emerging from beneath the object, which also had legs underneath and was obviously no car. It rose slowly, vertically and then laterally. Although he saw no windows or doors on the craft a red symbol was etched into the side (both Villas Boas and the Hills had referred to similar symbols inside the UFO).

Scared by the roar and aware of the danger of explosion from the nearby hut, Zamora scrambled round the car, hitting his leg as he did so, and then ran, keeping the car sandwiched between him to shield any blast. Then, suddenly, the roar stopped and he turned to look. The object had cleared the shack and was now moving silently away at great speed.

The officer reported the incident immediately and had the presence to sketch the insignia whilst fresh in his mind. His chief, Sergeant Chavez, had responded to his initial call and might have reached the area in time to see the object had he not made a wrong turn. As it was he got there to find the startled officer staring into the hollow where the scrub bush in the canyon was in smouldering fire.

Chavez went with Zamora into the canyon. Bushes were still smouldering but did not feel hot. There were also four indentations which seemed to fit landing marks. Something heavy had impressed into the canyon floor. Without a moment's hesitation, seeing the evidence and knowing the calibre of the witness (Zamora was a respected figure in the local church community) the sergeant launched an immediate enquiry, cordoning off the area and demarking the landing holes with circles of stone to allow photographs. Luckily an FBI agent was in the police station on other business that day and so the intelligence agencies, including the CIA, were also soon in on the hunt. The military called in Hynek to lead the scientific study of the site.

No trace of radiation, chemicals or propellant residue was found in the bush. However, some other witnesses appeared. Several people had called the police station to report the sound or flame but no names were recorded and by the time the significance of the incident was known back at base it was too late. But Hynek did speak to a petrol station owner who recalled a passing motorist just before he closed that day (at 6 p.m.) bemoaning 'low flying aircraft' in the area. Fourteen years later two men who claimed to be in that car were traced in another state and interviewed. One recalled seeing an egg shape emitting smoke that flew low over the car. The other only saw the smoke rising from scrubland.

UFO sceptics have tried to suggest this case is a hoax (often the last hope of the debunker when rational solutions fail). But it is interesting that Major Hector Quintanilla, the chief military investigator and a cynical sceptic, was more impressed by this report than any other. Knowing its significance he tried very hard to prove that it was a secret prototype vertical take off aircraft or a lunar landing module then being developed for the Apollo missions. His extensive efforts failed. He said: 'I've checked it out everywhere. All the way up to the top, even the White House ... Nothing.' Thirty years later it remains unsolved.

1965: Hidden Depths

The impact of a solid, reliable witness claiming to see aliens was to prove considerable. Suddenly investigators began to pay more heed to these reports and, particularly with the news about the Hill case and its hints of repressed memories masking a stranger encounter, also began to look more closely at the finer points for possible indications that they contained hidden depths.

Many wondered if the simple visits of the 1950s were gone, to become a more sinister sequence of events where human beings had replaced rocks and plants as prime focus of an alien's attentions, as seemed to be the case at Villa Santina, Italy and many other sightings from the previous decade. However, a case that occurred in France a year after Socorro was to suggest that there may be another way of viewing things.

The Basse-Alpes region of France, inland from Marseille, has over the years been at the heart of some of the strangest close encounters. It is set amidst rich farmland, more specifically, the fields between Valensole and Oraison are filled with lavender during the summer and to the local farmers it is a precious commodity. That is why forty-one year old Maurice Masse was upset when during June 1965 he kept finding clumps missing as if youths were vandalising his property.

At 5.45 a.m. on 1 July he sat by his immobile tractor having a smoke before starting work when he heard a curious whistling noise. At first he assumed it was a helicopter, as military craft had not infrequently set down on his land before. Wanting to ensure they did not damage his crop, he walked in the direction of the sound and saw an egg-like object resting on six legs that had landed in the midst of his field. Nearby were two figures which looked like youths, dressed in greenish/grey overalls. Determined to stop them he walked purposefully in their direction before realizing that these were not boys at all, but very strange creatures, only 4 feet tall, and with large pumpkin-shaped heads and pointed chins. The skin was white and the eyes slanted like a cat's. Apart from the smaller size this is a familiar description.

When he was within a few feet of the two beings one turned to face him and picked up a small tube-like object from a belt by its side. This emitted a beam which struck the farmer and he was immediately unable to move. However, he was clearly not paralysed as he could still breathe and remained completely conscious of all that was happening. The entities were communicating with one another issuing gutteral sounds.

Masse says that they then went into the object via a sliding door and the device took off with another whooshing sound. Once in the air and streaking away it vanished as if it simply 'popped' out of reality.

After the beam had been released it took some minutes for the farmer to regain his full ability to move, with muscles still struggling to coordinate. He saw that there were holes depressed into the lavender where the object had rested and later that day that what was like liquified mud in the middle of this depression had set hard.

Masse (he later came to believe very foolishly) told a local cafe owner what had happened, who suggested the police be called in. As a local resistance hero from the war and a member of a well respected family, the farmer did not wish to bother them with this, but the cafe owner reported it even so and from here the story quickly got out. The Masse family were hounded by the media and became pretty frustrated.

UFO investigators were more readily tolerated after the media were driven away. Samples from the site were analysed and an excessive level of calcium was the only strange thing they found. However, as photographs taken three years later show, only weeds would grow even then in the landing spot. The lavender would not take hold in the calcified soil.

The farmer suffered a severe attack of tiredness three days after the encounter and slept for fifteen hours. He also hinted at there being a hidden side to the story which he would not even share with researchers whom he came to trust, such as

Aime Michel. He reported that he knew the beings were friendly and had no hostile intent, but would only inform Michel: 'I did not tell all, but I have already said too much. It would have been better if I had kept it all to myself ... You have to have undergone it to understand it.'

Before his recent death, Michel confirmed to me that he believes from his conversations with the farmer that M. Masse went inside the UFO.

In 1965 when Michel first investigated the case he showed Maurice Masse a photograph of a model made of the object that had landed at Socorro. This case had only occurred fifteen months earlier in the USA and whilst not impossible it seems unlikely that Masse knew of the case before his sighting occurred. He certainly claimed not to do so. When he later saw the photograph he was extremely excited and believed for a moment that someone had filmed 'his' UFO. After the truth was explained he was delighted that a policeman in the USA was backing him up.

In August 1967 Michel also appears to have been the first person to tell Masse about the just revealed Hill abduction, then in print in English for under a year. The farmer's reaction is interesting: 'If these people say that they were forced it is not true ... They don't force anybody. If those people had said no, if they had said "I don't want to", *they* [presumably the entities] would have left them in peace.'

Michel tried to get an elaboration on how he knew all of this, but the farmer said that not even his wife knew the full story. 'I will die without telling anyone. Do not insist. But if I talk like this about those Americans it is because I *know* that's how it is.'

The reticence of Maurice Masse raised a disturbing possibility. Seemingly 'ordinary' close encounters of the third kind, as Dr Allen Hynek had termed such entity sightings, might contain a level of contact unsuspected by witness or investigator. If one looks again at some of the reports from the 1954 wave where the witness was paralysed by a beam of light we may ask if the encounter truly ended there? Or was it that nobody thought to look beyond this facade to whatever might lie within?

The similarities between Socorro and Velensole are extraordinary, even down to the way the witness was lured to the scene by a belief that young vandals might be at work. Some UFOlogists when they could compare these cases began to speculate whether alien contacts were being 'stage managed' for the benefit of witnesses, as if endeavouring to slowly build up a level of belief that fell just short of proof.

On cue, in December 1967, a Nebraska policeman had a close encounter with hidden overtones. It was one of the first probed under hypnosis as part of a government-funded scientific experiment at the University of Colorado. The witness, who was unaware of these ideas, said aliens told him that they intended we should 'believe in [them] some, but not too much.'

1973: Year of the Humanoids

There was a quiet spell for several years from the late 1960s. It was almost as if the lunar landings of 1969 and 1970 burst a bubble and UFOs were no longer quite the fantastic dream they once had been.

Indeed, the US government seized the initiative and with a clever bit of subterfuge actually shut down their twenty-two year old official study programme claiming UFOs had effectively gone away. Few knew that behind this pretence what were then secret (but are now public) documents show how intelligence agencies continued to keep in touch with 'UFO reporting channels' and research spin-off technology such as 'propulsion systems' (as some 1974 documents from the CIA's office of Scientific Research and Development argue).

Of course, UFO sightings continued to occur almost unabated, including those of the third kind. In fact waves were going on in far flung corners of the world from South America to the USSR, from where at the time almost no news of the hundreds of promising cases could filter out.

Nevertheless, alongside media indifference, especially in the USA which moulded global opinion, the sceptics warned that sightings had been nothing more than a 'space age' fad that we had now discarded.

However, UFOlogy had begun to see alarming signs of change. Whilst simple alien encounters were still occasionally taking place, those with elements of contact, time loss or hidden dimensions were obviously on the increase. Or, as some researchers suggested, the true extent of a problem that had always been there was at last being recognized.

Hypnosis was now being used by a few researchers, such as

psychologist and UFO investigator Dr Leo Sprinkle. He had become intrigued by a case that he had been called in to debunk for the US government. Sprinkle had completely failed to disprove it and began to suspect that as we scanned the universe for radio signals that might suggest other intelligences 'out there' a form of alien contact of a truly remarkable level was already taking place right underneath our noses all of the time.

Witnesses increasingly began to fear public ridicule and shunned the media, talking only to researchers on the grounds of confidentiality. This is a trend that has continued and for every alien contact that makes the press there are a dozen others, often just as interesting, where the witnesses simply do not want any public attention. This is a fact the sceptics often misrepresent, claiming publicity is the aim of witnesses.

Nonetheless, it was only a matter of time before one of the cases that trickled through the sieve reached the attention of the media on a quiet day. As a result they could announce that the aliens were back.

In October 1973 southern states of the USA were bombarded by UFO sightings. Many were impressive and it was impossible to keep them all from exposure as some witnesses inevitably wanted to talk. In one week between 11 and 18 October over 100 encounters took place in this area. They included a police officer photographing an entity in Alabama (see page 116) and a UFO with entities that landed on a road in front of a startled Georgia witness.

But the case which captured the attention of the world came mid evening on 11 October and involved two shipyard workers, forty-five year old Charles Hickson and eighteen year old Calvin Parker, who were fishing in some derelict land beside the river at Pascagoula, Mississippi.

They first heard a zipping noise and turned in time to see an oval object with blue lights encircling it which was descending to the ground nearby. They considered jumping into the water to escape but were instead frozen with fear as three strange entities floated out towards them. These beings did not conform to the pattern that UFOlogists (particularly in the USA) were now building up and for that reason the case was questioned by researchers. The entities were a similar size, 5 feet tall, but they were covered in a wrinkly skin (or suit?) with only slit eyes and pincer-like hands. Hickson did later suggest that he thought they were robots responding to commands from other unseen beings inside the object.

Two of these beings allegedly floated Hickson into the air and he passed out. He awoke inside a bright room where his colleague was present but was soon separated from him. Parker was still unconscious and Hickson says he never saw him again until both were deposited back by the river some minutes later. Parker himself confirmed the sighting of the UFO and beings but never professed any memory of going onboard.

Inside the UFO Charles Hickson was given some sort of inspection with the familiar-sounding eye-like device that was scanned all over his body. Other features found in other cases were also recorded, such as the fact that he felt no pain from the medical probing. Very little else was consciously remembered; although there do seem to be memory gaps.

Once back outside on the ground the two men debated what to do. They first went to the local paper, but it was closed. Then they called the local air base, who sent them to see the police. They reached there around 10.45 p.m. and were interviewed for some time. Sheriff Fred Diamond reported: 'They were scared to death and on the verge of a heart attack.' The chief investigating officer, Glen Ryder, concurred: 'If they were lying to me they should be in Hollywood.'

Unknown to either witness a hidden tape recorded all their conversations, even when left alone as they discreetly were at one stage. They continued to behave exactly as before. Indeed at one point, Parker was left completely alone without his companion. The tape records him praying: 'God help me. Please don't let me die.'

In the morning they were taken to Keesler Air Base near Biloxi for medical tests as this had the best set of local equipment. Nothing untoward was found but Colonel Robert Smith said that he believed: 'They suffered some type of frightening experience. We are convinced that they are not lying nor were they seeking publicity.'

But publicity is what they found. Indeed, as many other unsuspecting witnesses have discovered since then, when a story takes the reporters' fancy there is a siege mentality. In fact, the sheriff's office at Pascagoula took 2000 calls in three days from the world's media.

Forty-eight hours after the events Dr J Allen Hynek, now free from the US government ties and launching his own scientific UFO group (the Center for UFO Studies – which continues today in his name), and a hypnosis specialist from the University of California in Berkeley, Dr James Harder, both arrived in Mississippi and started work on the case. Harder did regress Hickson (Parker was 'too distressed') although he took a lot of persuading. The story was relived but the fear became so intense that hypnosis had to be terminated quickly as worries grew about Hickson's health. I have personally witnessed several similar situations where an abductee is so traumatised that doctors conclude it is too dangerous to go on.

Harder argued that this supported the reality of the case, adding that, 'a very strong feeling of terror is practically impossible to fake under hypnosis.' Hynek agreed that, 'There simply is no question in my mind that these men have had a very real, frightening experience.' But he was not prepared to be drawn on how physically real this was.

Two weeks later Charles Hickson was given a polygraph (lie detector) test at the Pendleton Detective Agency in New Orleans. These were all the rage at the time, although their use faded when major limitations were recognized. It is possible to lie with a bit of practice and, in any case, all they do is record what a person believes, not whether it is true. If someone sincerely thought they were Napoleon reborn, a lie detector test would confirm this, but would naturally prove nothing.

Hickson's test was conducted by a self-styled sceptic, Scott Glasgow, who reputedly tried hard to break the pretence he perceived. In the end he could only say, 'This s.o.b. is telling the truth.' But some sceptics have suggested that he was not properly qualified to judge this test and note how two years later (on advice from a lawyer) Hickson refused a properly supervised test at a police station.

Calvin Parker did not go to New Orleans for the polygraph. At the time he was in hospital suffering from severe nervous stress which allegedly had been directly attributable to the experience, however real or unreal this close encounter was in actual fact.

This case laid bare some of the critical issues that faced research into alien contact. Whilst many people said they believed Hickson and Parker, however much fear the men exhibited and what lie detector tests they passed, it was ultimately no more than a story which they told. There was no physical evidence to back it up. This allowed some UFOlogists, such as John Keel – one of the first to reject extraterrestrial visitors – to suggest that the two fishermen had experienced a vivid hallucination which was real to them but not real in fact.

Sceptics such as Philip Klass were not so charitable. He asks, for example, why nobody else in what was a very built-up area observed the landing UFO and entities during many minutes? Such questions still nag.

I should add that in 1987 I met Charles Hickson in Washington. He impressed me with his honesty and claimed that he turned down big money for selling movie rights. That was never the point, he mused.

1975: Smoke Behind the Fire in the Sky?

One of the problems arising from massive public exposure for a few alien encounters in the decade before 1975 was that it inevitably must have spawned some hoaxers who saw there was a commercial opportunity.

Generally speaking these are extremely rare situations. Anyone who has spent time with genuine witnesses to an incredible experience knows how the trauma they revive for research purposes and often have to live with for the rest of their lives is hardly ever conjured up by them to get into the paper. Five minutes in the spotlight is no compensation for what can be a lifetime in mental hell as they struggle to come to terms with what has happened to them. I have seen marriages end, careers vanish and mental and physical breakdowns result because once a witness lets the genie out of the bottle it can never be forced back in again.

The considerable majority (about 90 per cent) of all alien contacts are never reported outside the files of UFO groups. Indeed, I am privy to a couple of cases where I am sworn not to share the 'truth' even with a person's husband or wife. Of course, people are different in how they can handle these experiences. Just because they do not want to appear on a TV chat show does not mean they must be telling the truth and just because they are happy to tell (or even sell) their story publicly also does not mean that they made it all up for that very reason. As one UFO expert succinctly pointed out, even liars might have a close encounter.

Careful UFOlogists employ extensive investigation techniques, involving psychologists and similar practitioners, when evaluating alien contacts. Months of study can result. They have thirty years of knowledge about how real cases seem to manifest and have deliberately kept some important clues back from public exposure to act as a filter in future reports. However, all of this research cannot prevent some frauds slipping through. As we are dealing with a phenomenon where the ground rules are largely rewritten with each new case it is nigh impossible to make absolute judgements about what is taking place. We do not even know what we are trying to prove – from an alien visitation in constructed ships to a bizarre form of mental hallucination; merely two prime suspects.

In fact, with the realization that such stories were big news UFOlogists had to become more cautious than ever, reserving judgement on most cases in the absence of proof. I believe this is no bad thing.

In late 1975 a landmark case illustrates the problem very well. It was the last major alien contact to receive public exposure before the release of a movie then in the planning. That film, *Close Encounters of the Third Kind*, was a Steven Spielberg spectacular which was based upon the work of Dr J Allen Hynek (who himself has a cameo in the climactic scene). Although told as fiction, its bizarre title (using what for non UFOlogists was an obscure classification scheme for alien contact) alludes to the fact that Spielberg worked hard with the UFO movement to make it 'true to life'. Many of its scenes are based on actual cases and its images of pumpkin-headed small beings with whitish-grey skins and large eyes mirror the accumulating evidence with deliberation.

In 1977 and 1978 when this movie aired all over the world, becoming one of the highest grossing screenings of all time, its impact was enormous. Even more so than the newspaper serialization of the Hills' abduction a decade earlier, it ensured that millions, probably billions, of people understood what alien contacts were like. No case that has been investigated in its wake can be regarded as uncontaminated.

However, even the preceding events in the Sitgreave National Forest some 150 miles north of Phoenix, Arizona were not uncontaminated. At around 6.10 p.m. a seven man crew of forestry workers out logging near Snowflake saw a strange object behind trees as they wound their way home. But the movie of the Hills' 1961 abduction had premiered on TV a few days before.

The men (all aged between seventeen and twenty-eight)

were running late on a contract and risking penalty clauses, a fact touted by the sceptics as reason to invent a fantastic story. Indeed, 'fear of a return to the woods' was later suggested as one reason to drop the work; although this point is hotly disputed by the men. But the way in which motivations for a hoax were being sought out, not only by vigilante sceptics but also by some UFOlogists striving to be thorough, was a sign of times to come.

The object was like two pie cans stuck together glowing yellowy-white. The truck driver (Mike Rogers) pulled to a halt in a clearing to watch and colleague, twenty-two year old Travis Walton, leapt out and ran towards the UFO. The others, not surprisingly, were somewhat more reticent.

The men say Walton was suddenly hit by a beam of light that shot from the body of the beeping UFO (beeps are rare but form a part of the Hill abduction story). The forester was thrown backwards through the air by the ferocity of attack, glowing as if electrocuted. He crashed to the earth looking mortally wounded. The foresters are not proud of their response, but it may be understandable. They fled the scene in sheer desperation. Fifteen minutes later, having recovered their composure and seeing a light streak above their heads as if it were the UFO departing, Rogers drove back to pick up his stricken co-worker. Walton was not there.

The men returned to town and blurted out their claims to Navajo County Sheriff Marvin Gillespie. It is fair to say he suspected a hoax and ordered them all to take polygraph tests. They agreed and five passed them readily. The sixth could not be properly tested as he was too upset, but Philip Klass notes he was later charged with theft and so may have feared incriminating himself. Still undecided, Gillespie launched a search of the woods, using at first men on horseback and ultimately helicopters. No sign of anything untoward or of Travis Walton was found.

Of course, the story got out. This was not the first abduction case to be broadcast widely, but it was very different from any others before (and atypical of nearly all since) in that the abductee had quite literally disappeared. In fact Walton was missing for five days, until he called his home from a phone booth at the nearby town of Heber and his brother Duane went to pick him up.

Hardly surprisingly, the sheriff was more than a little

suspicious at this point that justice might have been obstructed and police time wasted. Walton was taken for questioning. He told the following story.

When he ran towards the UFO he was hit by a severe shock that knocked him out. The next thing Walton recalls is waking up in 'hospital' (i.e. a large well lit room) with a pain in his head. He soon reassessed his situation when three strange beings 'like a crowd of well-developed foetuses came towards him. They were about 5 feet tall wearing tan robes with white skins and mushroom-shaped heads. They had no hair and their eyes were very large. This has become a very standard description.

Walton attempted to fend off the beings but a human-looking man in a blue one-piece uniform arrived and took the abductee into another room like a planetarium, with 'stars' visible through the walls. He was eventually led outside into a sort of hangar with other UFOs inside.

The entities performed the now obligatory medical exam on Travis Walton as he lay on a table in the open, which is certainly unheard of in other cases. This ended when a mask was put over his face. He awoke on the highway near the phone booth unaware that five days had passed.

Police attempts to make progress hit real barriers. Both the UFO movement and the medical profession were seriously split over this case.

A psychiatrist, Dr Gene Rosenbaum, carried out a host of psychological tests on Walton and said, 'our conclusion, which was absolute, is that this young man is not lying.' On the other hand, the director of modern hypnosis at a Phoenix institute, Dr Lester Steward, bemoaned the fact that in his two hours with Walton the man refused to be hypnotised and kept demanding to see a medical doctor. Steward concluded the case was a hoax.

One UFO group publicly endorsed the case, another (the more sceptical Ground Saucer Watch, which specializes in exposing photographic frauds using computer enhancement techniques) concluded the opposite. Walton later attacked them in a UFO magazine, alleging they had ulterior motives for their decision (i.e., that he decided to cooperate with the other UFO group instead of them). He also attacked the media publicity saying, 'I haven't read one account of this that was totally correct'. As a result he went on to write his own book,

The Walton Experience, which appeared at the time of the Spielberg movie and, naturally, suggested to the sceptics other possible motivations for this case. Travis Walton and his six colleagues insist it was completely genuine.

Walton himself did 'pass' a lie detector test some months later, but as usual its validity was challenged by the sceptics. They also exposed a claim that Walton had failed a test paid for by a tabloid newspaper only a few days after his return from the UFO. They also allege this negative result was obscured by both the newspaper and the attending UFO group. UFOlogists involved in that contentious test defended Walton saying that he had failed this initial polygraph because he was still traumatised. Most who have met Walton consider him sincere.

As you can see, diagnosing truth about any individual alien contact claim was already hopelessly confounded and was not about to get any easier.

In 1993 Paramount Pictures resurrected this extraordinary case in a big budget movie called *Fire in the Sky*. I had the pleasure of working with them on a special 'UFO holiday to Britain' competition to aid promotion. In general the case was handled quite objectively. Walton himself even has a small role, asking where Travis is! Yet interestingly, screen writer Tracy Torme apologised to fellow UFOlogists for adding to the rather thinly recalled 'abduction' sequence many fictionalised elements, presumably for dramatic effect.

1980: The Education Programme

After the Walton case and follow-up book, the Spielberg movie and a huge overdose of media attention and pulp writing devoted to the UFO subject, abduction claims rose sharply in numbers. Straightforward alien sightings all but vanished and abductions became almost the norm.

Britain had its own year of the humanoids in 1976 and other parts of the world adopted such events gradually as the tide of encounters swept around the planet. The consistency between the reports was impressive, even though as you will see later there were major differences too.

In the mid 1970s a New York artist called Budd Hopkins began to work with psychiatrists on several long forgotten cases and concluded that using hypnosis you could discover hidden abductions lurking unsuspected in otherwise unprobed and decades-old reports. His book, *Missing Time*, at first made little impact but when his predictions seemed to come true, was reissued as a mass market paperback.

Hopkins suggested that abduction memories are often suppressed, either by the witness or deliberately by the aliens. He found clues that what he called 'screen memories' could replace true recall so that the witness never even knew about their encounter. Only very careful questioning revealed how there was something not quite right about a case.

For instance, a witness might recall seeing a UFO and how it vanished suddenly, but then have an odd memory of seeing rabbits surrounding the car. There would probably be other hints, eg., a severe phobia of driving down a certain stretch of road causing the witness to divert miles in future trips. Hopkins figured that this and imagery such as the rabbits were a screen that was masking a more traumatic memory and, via hypnosis, helped the witness recover this from their subconscious.

Of course, sceptics were quick to point out that to an extent this was manipulation of the evidence, effectively manufacturing abduction stories out of whole cloth. It all turned on whether you were prising out hidden memories or stimulating fantasies. We still do not know the truth.

It was to be some years before any UFOlogist even saw that such fundamental questions had to be asked. The drama of dozens of abductions appearing like magic when you probed otherwise mundane cases was far too great for many to abandon. Eager UFOlogists simply thrilled to their new toy and went on collating (or, as some feared, creating) the evidence.

Of course, for those UFOlogists, notably in the USA, who accepted the literal reality of these claims this represented a dramatic new phase of UFO activity. The aliens had begun a widespread campaign of abduction and the only important thing to do was to figure out what 'they' were up to. This reinforced the concept of a government cover-up, because it was widely held to be untenable that such a massive 'hidden invasion' would go unrecognized by the American authorities. Eventually speculation even reached the point where it was concluded by some that there may be collusion between governments of the major world powers and the aliens.

In December 1980 I was honoured to be invited to brief politicians from the Lords and Commons in Britain's Palace of

Westminster. In this high-powered debate a senior figure told me of an 'education programme' he sensed was underway. Later I discovered the same idea was fed out to several other UFOlogists. The claim was that the public were being gradually acclimatized to the reality of alien contact by a carefully arranged series of tableaux or displays, big cases that were allowed to generate lots of publicity but no absolute proof. Possibly powers that be smoothed the way for big budget media and cinema ventures to express the UFO dream on screen. Overall, there would be a slow increase in the amount and calibre of the evidence until it persuaded many that benevolent aliens were already here as an inevitable consequence. When the official revelation was ultimately made, people would be ready and there would be no mass panic. Frankly the claim struck me as absurd.

In the meantime, as was also pointed out, there were sound reasons for governments to keep the truth quiet. Nobody wanted to admit to a phenomenon they could not control and western powers were fighting one another to try to duplicate UFO technology by learning how these things do what they do. As such, it was positively beneficial to maintain a public illusion that there were no UFOs at all. This stifled private scientific enterprise and ensured that the only research carried out was being carefully supervised by the intelligence community.

Only two weeks after I first heard this bizarre concept in Britain's corridors of power what many still regard as the country's greatest ever alien contact case arrived. It did so in such a way that it amplified many of these concepts and, because of the way it fell into my lap, had me rather egotistically wondering if it was somehow stage managed for my benefit. I doubt that was true, but I may have been part of some grand design that also involved many others.

The case is immensely complicated and I have written two full books describing the years of effort that I and several others have expended trying to figure out exactly what took place. My book *From Out of the Blue* (Berkeley, 1993) gives the up-to-date position.

It centred on Rendlesham Forest, a huge pine wood in Suffolk to the east of Ipswich. Two NATO air bases nestle in the trees, RAF Bentwaters and Woodbridge, both being leased by the British government to the USA and staffed almost entirely by US forces.

We know that late on the night of 25/26 December 1980 a dazzling light crossed the sky and was seen by several villagers. It was also apparently tracked on radar at a British base near Norwich and 'went down' near Woodbridge. Around this time security police officers on patrol saw something fall out of the sky and went on foot into the forest to investigate. Here they saw a cone-like object on the ground and a close encounter resulted until it shot away.

At dawn some indentations were found in the ground as if created by the tripod legs seen beneath the UFO and a huge hole was smashed through the treetops as if something heavy had crashed from the sky. During what seems to have been an unofficial investigation the next night further lights were seen by several senior officers and this event was tape recorded 'live'. The UFOs upset farm animals and were chased through the woods by Uncle Sam's men. Beams of light reputedly shot out and passed through trees and a truck as if they were transparent. The US airmen not surprisingly got very concerned and the tension can be clearly heard in their voices using words like, 'Now we observe what appears to be a beam ... ah ... coming down towards the ground ... This is unreal.'

Given evidence, such as this tape, the testimony of many witnesses and official documentation squeezed out via the American freedom of information act after years of denials from the British government, this is obviously an important case. However, what makes it even stranger is that a couple of the witnesses say they saw aliens – small, large-headed, big-eyed, indeed the now standard 'American' type – floating suspended beneath the object in shafts of light. Other witnesses say that it was as if government sources were unsurprised by the incident – in fact, almost as if the whole thing were expected at the very top. One commented that the reaction of ordinary airmen seemed of great interest. There is also evidence that at least one of the airmen lost a period of time during the sighting and when he recovered was elsewhere in the forest entranced by what had taken place. This hints at the possibility of an abduction to some UFO researchers.

All those who have come forward to tell their story – from security patrolmen to the deputy base commander who signed the official report – appear to be sincerely recording what to them must have been an amazing and baffling experience. They do not know what they encountered and have wisely refrained from jumping to conclusions. But the feeling of an alien stage show lasting several hours pervades the unreality of this case.

Equally hard to fathom out is how the facts emerged as readily as they did. There was a whole series of escalating revelations.

Two weeks after it happened one security officer befriended a local researcher and told her the whole story, allowing her to share it with a colleague and then a few weeks later with me.

A month after it happened the case came to me via a roundabout route. I was told of the radar tracking and, most strangely, how USAF intelligence had arrived at the base to secure tapes of that tracking for future analysis, telling RAF men and civilian workers precisely what went on in the forest in justification for this request. There seems no need for this to have occurred. Why breach security so easily?

Eventually letters of admission from the British government, never to be repeated 'on the record' statements from senior figures in Britain and America and the 'live' tape, which was denied for over two years on both sides of the Atlantic and then sent by a military commander with no strings attached, all gradually escalated the strength of this case.

It was almost as if people who would normally be prevented from talking by official secrecy were allowed to do as they liked on this case, contrary to all expectations. As a result a specific impression about the incident emerged, probably without any witness intent. It even made front page banner headlines on the most widely read newspaper in Britain and from here much of the rest of the world.

Unbeknown to all the airmen, colonels, deputy base commanders, full commanders and the investigators, struggling to piece their tales together, we must wonder if there was someone at the very top in Britain or the USA who might have been manipulating the way in which the story entered the public domain. In any event the result was its gradual assimilation amongst the general public.

If the education programme is more than paranoia or fantasy, this timely case fits well. But I am aware of my pivotal role within the release of the data. Was I fed that line so conveniently at just the right moment as mere speculation, significant information or *attempted dis*information?

1987: Fun and Games in Florida

Alien contact took a further dramatic step when Whitley Strieber, a noted and respected horror writer, read one of my books bought for him as a Christmas present in 1985. In this I described the early work by Hopkins and others to uncover hidden abductions. Strieber quickly recognized that the cases we were discussing related to certain images within his mind, the status of which he had been unable to determine.

Strieber contacted Hopkins, who lived nearby, then worked with a hypnotherapist and eventually (in 1987) his book *Communion* emerged, relating his personal attempt to come to terms with these abduction-like experiences. The power of Strieber's writing helped ensure that the story became the most widely read UFO book in history, selling millions of copies around the world. A movie starring Christopher Walken appeared in 1989 and although Strieber had a pretty uneasy relationship with UFOlogy, his accounts further ensured that almost nobody in the developed world could be unfamiliar with what an alien contact was like.

A few months after this story had featured on TV chat shows across America a man in the small Florida town of Gulf Breeze submitted some photographs to the local paper. Mr Ed, as he was anonymously referred to by UFOlogists until his real name, Ed Walters, was revealed, eventually explained how he was observing these colourful objects in the sky and taking regular polaroid shots of them. In the wake of the Strieber story this was too good for the media to pass up and news outlets besieged Gulf Breeze in a stream that was slow to abate. In 1993 there are still occasional 'specials' broadcast from this town, which has rapidly become the UFO tourist centre of the world.

Ed Walters's photographs were unusually graphic, possibly the most visually stunning since Adamski's thirty years earlier. They resembled colourful Chinese lanterns. He photographed the object in the sky, partly behind trees, firing a beam of light towards him and in one case above his head as he shakes his fist at it whilst wrapped only in a towel.

The photographer alleged stranger encounters of a contact nature as well. Once the UFO supposedly descended onto the road in front of his truck and he had to scramble away, taking one classic picture of the object just five or ten feet above the road surface beaming down a light onto the ground.

In another incident a being around 4 feet tall, with a stick-like implement and other similarities with Strieber's story appeared in his garden and was scared away, but no photograph was obtained.

UFO groups soon became embroiled in the controversy. Some openly disputed the credibility of this case. Others brought out their big guns to support the witness. Photographic analyses were published supporting the authenticity of the case, others attacking it, but several prominent American UFOlogists, such as optical physicist, Dr Bruce Maccabee, and abduction guru Budd Hopkins, supported the case in another well publicised book that Ed Walters sold worldwide in 1989.

The critics of the case were delighted when what looked to be plans for a model UFO were found in Ed Walters' house after he moved and someone came forward to claim he had helped Ed organize a hoax. Walters denied this and researchers who had backed him noted that the evidence could have been planted and pointed out how the story did not stand or fall on the testimony of one man. Various other photographs were taken and many other residents of Gulf Breeze claimed to have seen the UFOs.

In May 1992 Bruce Maccabee himself video filmed a strange object in the town and two TV cameras, one a sophisticated colour camera, the other a long focus black and white model, captured the event simultaneously. In situations such as this there was no question of a hoax by the photographers. They clearly saw something. But this did not rule out the possibility that third parties were 'creating' UFOs, e.g. by building small hot air balloons and launching them over the bay, a suspicion that a few UFOlogists have expressed about recent sightings. It must be admitted that once an area becomes so attractive to tourists then occasionally it may tempt somebody to enhance that reputation for personal reasons.

On the other hand, those who had followed the concept of the education programme noticed how it was as if the phenomenon had moved up another notch towards global acceptability, by parading now almost nightly and to order in one small town. Certainly in Gulf Breeze photographers were sometimes going home with more than holiday snaps.

1992: Full Circle

The alien abduction phenomenon shows no sign of ending and its international appeal is spreading.

Although the small, bald headed creatures have been a staple of American UFO lore for twenty years the same is not true in other countries (see page 75). However, after the publication of Hopkins' and Strieber's books expressing this image before millions, cases of that type began to appear elsewhere and to increase in number.

Prior to 1987 in Britain there were a fraction of the number of American abductions per head of population. Less than a quarter involved the small bald headed entities. After these books appeared the next five years brought almost as many cases as the last four decades put together and over half of these involved the American standardized alien.

One can read this a number of different ways, but obviously the fact is not without significance.

By 1992, when *Intruders*, the TV mini-series based on Budd Hopkins' work, reached there, Australia was one of the last almost abduction-free zones with only a few cases reported to the largely more sceptical community of investigators. Using the TV mini-series publicity to seek out cases, unsurprisingly they flooded in (often older cases not yet reported) and many of them had imagery that was closely related to the American data.

Possibly part of the reason for the overwhelming focus of abduction cases within the USA (over two-thirds of them are from that country) is that there were different expressions of the alien theme elsewhere. In Britain, for example, the 1980s were just as much dominated by the crop circles as American UFOlogy was swamped by abductions.

These curious swirled patterns found overnight in crop fields suggested to some that a 'craft' had descended from above. We have good reason to believe they have existed for centuries, but the phenomenon was only recognized in summer 1980 and active research began then. By 1992 hundreds of circles and patterns were appearing in southern English fields and tourists were coming thousands of miles to look at them.

There were three main schools of thought from very early days. The sceptics believed them to be manmade hoaxes and in many cases, particularly with the more absurd designs, this is clearly what they were. A group of scientists and (to many people's surprise) British UFOlogists promoted the view that atmospheric forces were the cause, and for the simpler designs considerable support for that possibility was mounted. However, neither of these views had the attraction of the third belief system, which spawned best-selling books, active research teams and generated huge publicity all over the world. This was that the circles were a form of contact; a new method of expressing alien communication.

These questions can be found debated elsewhere (*Crop Circles: A Mystery Solved* by Jenny Randles and Paul Fuller, Hale, 1993). However, it was only a matter of time before circles and alien abductions were merged into a common theme by claimed events. This was to occur in 1992.

In fact, the circles reached Hungary for the first time that summer. Mostly they were very simple and not the fantastic designs grabbing the attention of the media everywhere else. This former repressed eastern bloc state had just been freed into newfound democracy and embraced both crop circles and UFOlogy in rapid succession. During 1991 and 1992 books by Strieber, Hopkins and myself were translated into the language and hit the bookstores and the media circuit. As a result, this society cycled through the changes that had taken many years elsewhere, opening up all the debates and exposing the 10 million inhabitants of this charming country to all the amazing stories and ideas that America and the rest of Europe had assimilated across several decades.

Hungary quickly took on board its own cases of both the circles and abductions and from the resultant mix produced what may be the first of a new hybrid (an intriguing metaphor under the circumstances).

The first abductions appeared in late 1991. All the known cases (by late 1992) involved young people aged between eighteen and twenty-four from the professional classes (eg., an airline pilot and a nurse). The female nurse, for example, told UFOlogist Karoly Hargitai how under hypnosis she recalled being scanned by a probe inside a UFO where the small grey-skinned beings took body fluid and blood samples under the supervision of taller, more human-like entities. There were gynaecological elements to her story also.

Then at Szekszard, near a field where crop circles in the form of a 'solar system' manifested soon after, a woman in a car saw a big light come towards her and then she lost all consciousness. She recovered inside the car but right in the middle of a field and surrounded by long fallen snow. There were no tracks to indicate how the car could possibly have got into the field. Both engine and lights had failed.

The woman stumbled towards a distant light which proved to be a security guardpost. Here she found that her leg was covered in blood. She was driven to hospital having symptoms of heat and dizziness on the way. Fearing a heart attack the doctor examined her and was amazed to see her body covered in burn-like wounds. The police were called in and they found her car door handle welded shut. It had melted through extraordinary heat. The woman's injuries also comprised unusual puncture marks and a strange rash over exposed parts of her skin.

The woman became pregnant. This was confirmed by her doctor. However, she then began to 'spot' blood, a possible symptom of a spontaneous abortion. She was rapidly sent for an ultrasound and on this an image of an abnormally developed foetus allegedly appeared. The doctor told her that there was no baby after all and insisted on an operation to clean her out. This was later confirmed to the UFOlogist but Hargitai says the ultrasound recording does show that there was a foetus present.

Whether proof of this case will ever emerge remains to be seen. Several similar 'phantom pregnancy' cases have been reported in the USA and as yet none have any hard medical evidence to support them. It represents the latest phase of the gynaecological element of the abduction experience which some UFOlogists see as an alien experiment.

Whilst such overt blending of crop circle message and abduction is so far unique, it is not the only link. In 1980 one of Britain's first abductions (involving a police officer at Todmorden, West Yorkshire) left a swirled circle on a wet road surface. This has close similarities with later crop circles. Even more dramatic, a 1988 case where a woman in a car lost several hours and awoke to find her vehicle covered in mud, took place at an isolated but intense hot spot near Daresbury in Cheshire where various remarkable time loss cases have occurred. In August 1990 a crop circle (rare in Cheshire) formed in the very field just yards from the spot where that 1988 'abduction' encounter was alleged.

Part One: Summary

As you can see, claims of alien contact have grown in complexity from a very simple beginning. There have been many escalations throughout the past half century. We shall look in more detail at motivations and activities by the aliens in these supposed contacts and how they agree and disagree with one another around the world. But it must already be apparent that no case stands alone as the ultimate proof. All to some extent depend upon events that by now have a high public profile.

Cases such as the 1992 Hungarian abduction reflect the current archetypal image according to the latest revelations from Budd Hopkins. Female abductees have been reporting ova samples taken from them for several years. But now the trend is that they are told by their captors that these are for use in genetic experiments to create hybrid babies. These are supposedly implanted back into the womb during an abduction and then somehow removed before maturity of the foetus in a subsequent abduction. Some of the abductees even claim to have seen the alien/human hybrids after they are born (presumably in an alien place).

To some American UFOlogists this hybridization pro-gramme is the point of the abduction and makes sense of the sampling and kidnapping that has gone on since 1957. To more sceptical-minded people it is an indication of how once a single incident is reported in a big way (eg., via a popular book or TV film) others will describe similar incidents so as to conform to the accepted pattern. These need not be conscious fabrications. They could result from whatever process causes the abduction to develop within society or the mind. But if they are believed as literal fact by UFOlogy and promoted as the latest phase, this will inevitably generate more cases that seem to emphasize the pattern.

There is some evidence for this process. Aliens who smelled of cinnamon have been reported several times since Strieber described his encounter this way. Are subsequent cases confirmatory proof or do they reflect another unknown pattern at work? The truth is we do not know. But we do finally realize that we need to ask such questions.

PART TWO

An Alien Menagerie

By now you may have reasonably concluded that aliens appear in only one or two shapes and sizes. But you would be mistaken. There is a fascinating variety to some reports and a look at the more unusual differences can offer clues as to what may be going on.

Monstrous Creatures

As noted earlier, monstrous beings fill mass market science-fiction horror films but are very rare in the actual records of alien contact. However, there is a category of creature that has appeared on a number of occasions and which might be likened to a giant hairy bird.

Interestingly, these bizarre reports tend to come from 'window areas', which are regions around the planet where UFO sightings have gone on for centuries and focus at an intensity far beyond the normal.

For example, the Preston Brook/Daresbury area south of Warrington has already been mentioned for its association with abduction, missing time, car stops and crop circles. In fact, this small area, birthplace to the author of *Alice in Wonderland* and *Through the Looking Glass* (an apt coincidence) has spawned more alien contacts than anywhere in Europe.

In 1966 two fishermen saw something swoop low down in the early hours and almost sink a barge upon the canal. It was described as an enormous bird, larger than a man, with glowing eyes. The event took place just 200 yards from where a crop circle and unrelated abduction would occur years later. Even TV personality Fred Talbot has since reported odd sounds and suction forces whilst travelling on a barge in this area.

At the same time as the giant bird episode occurred in Cheshire a similar creature was terrorizing Point Pleasant, West Virginia in the USA. So many reports of it were received that the local media nicknamed it 'Mothman', for it did resemble a cross between a moth and a man, covered in hair and with a huge wingspan. It was also seen to fly.

On 15 November 1966 Roger Scarberry and Steve Mallette were driving with their wives down a dirt road near an old power plant when they saw a 7 foot tall winged dark shape with eyes that glowed coal-fire red. It swooped out towards them as they shot away at great speed. The witnesses all insist that it paced the car above and behind them as if some avenging nemesis! Not surprisingly they went straight to the police who launched an investigation but could not find the entity.

Countless UFO sightings tagged alongside reports of this 'Mothman' and journalist John Keel got his teeth into an affair which he later turned into an extraordinary book (*The Mothman Prophecies*).

The reason for this odd title is that he saw right away how the UFO and creature sightings often brought in their wake all manner of paraphysical manifestations, such as poltergeist outbreaks within the homes of victims. It was as if the experience had unleashed psychic energies within their lives. Precognitions were also involved, such as apparent entity prophecies about an event when the president turned on the Christmas lights in Washington during December 1967. However, on the predicted date instead of such a revelation, the bridge that ferried traffic across the Ohio River into the by now haunted town of Point Pleasant collapsed, taking with it many cars and trucks and claiming the lives of several of the witnesses to this notorious outbreak of alien activity.

Based upon such investigations Keel concluded that there was more to alien contact than meets the eye and shunned the popular extraterrestrial theory in favour of an inter-dimensional or paraphysical solution. His ideas found little favour with UFOlogists, but in 1992 he confirmed that subsequent events have only proven him right and he is more certain than ever that cases such as the 'Mothman' should be 'studied and not ignored because they do not fit the cosy pattern of friendly alien scientists which the UFO groups seem to desire'.

These beings are still around. In 1991 there were reports from the frozen Taiga in the former Soviet Union of a giant flying bat-like man.

Energy Forms

It was the partly overcast morning of 9 November 1979, amidst a mini UFO flap. Forestry foreman Bob Taylor had been working since 7.45 a.m. amidst Dechmont Woods, Lothian, Scotland and had taken his mid-morning break at home. He drove his pick-up back into the woods, parked it and then set off on foot with his dog to check some trees in a clearing not far from the new M8 motorway. He estimates entering this about 10.30.

In front of his eyes he was startled to see a Saturn-shaped object seemingly just above the ground and coloured a translucent grey.

The device had a rim across the middle carrying what appeared to be little rotors and several portholes around the edge. Yet its most remarkable feature was that it was fading in and out of reality as if only partly formed. At times the background could be seen through it. He likened it to an attempt to camouflage itself into the surrounding trees and sky. Taylor is convinced the object was really there, not a vision, and some evidence collected from the case certainly supports this.

Two strange beachball sized 'things' suddenly came towards him from the direction of the 'craft'. These were, as he put it, 'like sea mines with about six legs attached thereto'. They rolled at some speed across the ground, but with part of them never touching, making a kind of suction noise (later said to be akin to a vacuum cleaner on wet soil). Within moments they had reached his side and were at his feet. A terrible pungent odour struck him down, he felt a burning sensation on his chin, pressure at the top of his thighs and fell forward towards the object, as if being tugged. At the same moment he crashed to the ground and lost consciousness.

Bob Taylor recovered an unknown time later (careful reconstruction showed it to be about twenty minutes). He found himself on the damp earth hearing the barking of his dog. When he looked up there was no sign of the object. (He later speculated that the dog may have scared the things away.)

Bob felt extremely weak and nauseous, had a burning feeling in his throat and was unable to utter any sounds for some minutes.

The forester struggled to drag himself half erect and along the ground towards his truck. Here he tried to radio for help, but was quite incapable. As the physical symptoms gradually faded he attempted to drive away but his coordination was in tatters and he ran the truck into the mud at the side of the track where it got stuck firm. He then staggered home in a very shocked state, telling his wife what had occurred.

Mary Taylor recalls seeing her husband tottering up the steps and immediately realized that something was wrong. He told her 'I've been attacked' and when she naturally interpreted this as in more earthly terms he elaborated, 'No – by a spaceship thing'. She says that he was pale and exhausted and very dirty, so she immediately ran him a bath. His trousers were torn and he kept complaining about a vile smell in his nose and mouth. She called a doctor and Malcolm Drummond, his boss.

At the site some unusual marks were found and immediately cordoned off for later police study. They comprised two runner-like tracks and a large number of indentation holes surrounding them. These were consistent with imprints from a heavy landed object and holes dug by the two spiked balls as they came towards the witness. Of course, other interpretations were feasible, such as heavy plant machinery, but checks indicated that none had been in this location recently and in any case further tracks leading into the clearing would have been visible.

Dr Gordon Adams' report is particularly interesting. He confirms that he examined the witness in his home about noon. He did have a graze on his thigh but no abnormal blood pressure or other signs of injury; although Taylor said that he had a headache. The forester had been treated for meningitis in 1965 and on 3 July 1979 had reported to his GP with recurrent headaches. As a precaution Dr Adams sent him to hospital for tests but he was released after a week when nothing was found.

In view of this precedent the GP again suggested that Bob Taylor take himself to casualty, have more tests and be seen by a specialist. The witness reluctantly agreed to this but, as he and his wife planned a weekend in England, they left the hospital without examination after getting fed up by the lengthy waiting time that is all too common in such non-emergency situations.

Meanwhile the story leaked out, from a police or forestry source, as many people from both were at the site that afternoon. Bob was reluctant to talk, but did confirm the story and then left on his trip, glad of the escape. Most media sources exaggerated or got facts incorrect and it was falsely stated in some quarters that he had 'fled' or was under intense treatment in hospital. On 14 November Dr Adams visited again and found him well but advised an appointment with a neurologist. Taylor declined.

Lester Knibb and Jennifer Hendry of the CID forensic laboratories in Edinburgh conducted tests on the trousers, finding only that the tears were caused by a mechanical force pulling outward and therefore consistent with Bob Taylor's account. The conclusion of the police enquiry was that they had no reason to doubt the witness's story and could find no source for the report, presumably other than the one which the forester described.

An excellent study was made by Steuart Campbell for the British UFO Research Association, with cooperation from the police and Taylor's co-workers. Various scientists checked the evidence (eg., chemist Dr Tom Straiton and geologist Dr Colin Farrow) but samples from the site (and comparison samples from a nearby molehill) showed nothing abnormal. The witness was even given several vials of gas to smell to try to isolate the smell, with sulphur dioxide coming closest. Dr Patricia Hannaford sought out possible medical causations, noting that the best fit was with a one-off epileptic seizure which often brings unusual smells as well as unconsciousness. Taylor's medical history shows no prior (or, as of 1993, subsequent) attacks but his earlier meningitis may be relevant.

In the end Campbell suggested the not unreasonable theory that a rare electrical phenomenon akin to ball lightning may have been encountered and somehow triggered a temporary seizure. The witness never accepted this idea and several years later Campbell developed the more unusual theory that the object might be an optical mirage of a star or planet, normally invisible against a daylight sky and perhaps just below the horizon at the time. Few UFOlogists warmed to this possibility; although Campbell (writing sceptically on UFOs and no longer a BUFORA investigator) has published various articles on this same theme applying it broadly to other classic UFO cases such as famous abductions.

Sixty-one year old Bob Taylor lived and worked in Livingston new town a few miles west of Edinburgh. Everyone who knew him testified to his sincerity and all those who met him (myself included) have had no serious doubts that he was reporting only what he saw. He has never courted publicity and has sought to make nothing from his experience.

The case has a unique position in UFO lore, not only because of the strangeness of the entities (if indeed that is what they were) but also because it was treated as a physical assault by the Lothian police and therefore given an extensive criminal investigation. This is certainly unprecedented for any 'alien contact' case in Britain, and possibly for one anywhere else in the world.

In a science-fiction TV series such as *Star Trek*, a common type of alien is an 'energy form' without a specific body. This instructive case is regarded as Scotland's most significant alien contact and suggests something different from the normality of alien humanoids.

In 1992 it became the first location to be honoured by the local council when they placed a plaque at the site demarking where the encounter had taken place some thirteen years before.

Unfortunately, nine months later that plaque was abducted by unknown forces (no doubt terrestrial ones) and mysteriously vanished overnight!

The case certainly opens up the alien contact mystery to different solutions, suggesting that the experience may be occurring in more of a visionary than an absolute sense; although most researchers presume the latter. But on the other hand it may suggest that entities are like organisms such as amoeba in nature. Did Bob Taylor visualize a raw state 'energy form' out of which emerged his rather less standard observation?

It is also highly interesting to note that Bob Taylor says he was later tricked into undergoing hypnotic regression without being told this was to occur. This was not through any UFO group or investigator. However, he relived the story, complete with its emotions, but added no details, eg., of a hidden abduction. Despite the pressure he was placed under he was not coerced into conjuring up a phantom kidnap memory.

Shape Shifters

That aliens might not be all that they seem was certainly hinted at by the Livingston encounter. But it is even more apparent from a remarkable investigation carried out in rural Wales. Here the entities resemble so called 'shape-shifters' in ancient mystical lore.

Trevor was on holiday with his parents and brother in central Wales. It was 22 July 1975 and they were in Dovey Vale near the town of Machynlleth, Powys, looking at a holiday home for possible future visits.

By now it was early evening, but still bright, and Trevor took himself up a small incline near Wylfa Hill. At the summit he was astonished to be confronted by an amazing sight and hid behind a rocky outcrop to watch.

There was a large round object on the ground surrounded by lights studded into the base and separated by grooves of some sort. The lights were of colours he could simply not describe. A see-through dome was atop the base with another spectacular light of unknown hue. There was also a piece of 'equipment' in the middle of the dome and surrounding this two creatures of the most incredible order.

The beings were mostly shapeless and looked like lumps of jelly (jello) or plasticine. They were translucent white and were filled with small circles like blood corpuscles (the boy called them doughnuts). As Trevor watched the 'beings' he could see that they were permanently changing shape with only the central part remaining intact. It seems as if they were in a constant state of flux.

Suddenly a panel opened slowly in the right hand side of the object and one of the odd looking 'jellymen' started to float towards it and disembark. Trevor was understandably horrified and fled down the hill.

He recalls blurting out something to his father (who says that he calmly spoke, 'You won't believe me – come on!') and pointing up the hill. His father took no obvious interest, but did see the boy lie down to look at something beyond the crown. Inexplicably the teenager says he ran back up the hill, possibly expecting his father to follow. Upon arrival there the vision was still present; although the hatch was now shut and the jellymen were back inside. A noise like a soft engine was heard.

It was at this point that the truly extraordinary was set to occur.

The light atop the object and inside the base began to glow and pulsate in a strange mixture of colours that exactly matched the scenery (ie., grass green, earth brown, sky blue). This morass of colour expanded to envelop the object and the beings inside and it simply went into the background like a chameleon camouflages itself to hide from a predator. After a few moments it just was not there any more.

One of the most convincing aspects of this case is the way in which Trevor struggled to put into words this indescribable process. It was evident that no language covers such an experience and every metaphor does not do justice to the reality.

His father now saw Trevor rush down the hill, stumbling and collapsing at his feet. He was now 'really petrified' and dragged his father up the slope. Nothing was visible but his father did hear an odd noise like the wind rushing through the grass.

The boy's parents admit that they wrote this story off as a young man's vivid imagination and thought no more about it; although their son insisted it was true. Then, twenty-four hours later, Trevor suddenly lost the power of speech. As his brother was suffering from a sore throat both were taken to see a local doctor who concluded that they must have tonsilitis and Trevor recovered quite quickly.

The family returned home and Trevor went back to school. But in mid-August he lost the sight in his left eye. He also began to suffer extreme insomnia. Indeed, for six weeks he barely slept at all, insisting on staying downstairs all night. Trevor's worried parents took him to see various doctors. An eye specialist found no physical cause and transferred the case to a psychiatrist. The effects were worsening and moving from one eye to the other. For a time he lost the sight of both eyes, before things improved. It took many months of treatment to bring him through and even upon investigation three years later he was not fully recovered. It was thought that the mental scars would take a long time to heal.

As to the cause of the physical symptoms, no obvious source was found. The doctor, and a psychologist, apparently concurred that they were classic examples of psychosomatic responses – hysterical blindness can result in teenagers if they see something so horrific they wish to try to shut it out.

In such cases the trigger is normally a traumatic family episode, but it is by no means medically inconceivable that

Trevor's mind had simply overloaded on this remarkable experience and reacted by generating the physical symptoms.

Whilst some will suppose that the whole episode must be a hallucination that postdated the youth's 'breakdown', thus being a symptom of it, not a cause, it should be noted that neither expert thought this probable and there were no evident prior indications of the onset of disorder. Trevor was a normal, happy boy, doing well at school.

This case was one of the most disturbing to emerge in February 1978 when I had worked with the *Daily Express*. They had run a UFO bureau to preview the soon to be released movie *Close Encounters of the Third Kind*. Such a startling letter from a teenager in Essex was shocking. Recognizing the significance of this case I asked local investigator Andy Collins to look into it and he did so, along with colleague (and himself a victim of alien contact) Barry King and also psychologist Graham Phillips.

There have been many other cases where the UFO has appeared or disappeared instantly without apparent motion and some where this blending in and out of reality has been described. The presence of entities in such a circumstance is less common; although the incidents within Rendlesham Forest, Suffolk, in December 1980 did later bring forth some similar testimony from US Airman Larry Warren who spoke of strange distortion effects on the object's surface and how the craft materialized on the spot from out of an explosion of light. Others told of a mist or fog from which the UFO simply emerged.

An entity case from Medway in Kent in August 1980 also involved a woman who saw two humanoids inside a bubble-like and camouflaged object which instantly materialized out of mist or fog that was emitting a sickly odour.

Phantasms

Occasionally it can be difficult to separate the more amorphous UFO encounters from ghostly apparitions. That is certainly true in this case.

Ken was a thirty-eight year old service engineer heading home to Warrington, Cheshire, after a union meeting. It was about 11.30 p.m. on 17 March 1978 and he had taken a short cut down a then isolated and quiet road passing beside the UK Atomic Energy centre at Risley.

Suddenly a figure appeared ahead, as if a jaywalker courting disaster. It was coming down the steep embankment and leaning forward in a way that I found impossible to duplicate under Ken's directions. It seemed to have arms sprouting from the top shoulders and was eerie white. Two eyes were the only facial features.

The thing stopped in the middle of the road to face Ken, who had slowed his vehicles to a halt. Beams of light now poured from its eyes and struck the driver's hands as they gripped the steering wheel. He told me how he felt: 'My head swimming with thoughts ... I felt very odd ... like two enormous hands pressing down on me from the top. The pressure was tremendous. It seemed to paralyse me. I could only move my eyes. The rest of me was rigid.'

Finally, the figure simply moved on and walked straight through a fence into the grounds of the atomic plant, climbing a slight incline and vanishing as if it were a ghost. This stunned the witness.

He drove home and told his wife. She gave Ken a strong drink and took him straight to see the police, who went back to the site and checked the fence, finding it 10 feet high and impossible to scale. Both they and the plant security were concerned about intruders and searched thoroughly for any hole. There was none.

This encounter had many serious repercussions. Ken suffered sunburn on the exposed part of his fingers. His watch stopped at 11.45 p.m. Most serious of all, the very expensive radio fitted to his vehicle to receive calls from base failed when he came to use it forty-eight hours later.

Company engineers found that there had been a massive power surge (probably through the aerial) which had caused the diodes and capacitors to blow. It was too badly damaged to be repaired and had to be replaced at some cost.

There was also some evidence that deeper memories might have been involved. On two occasions during the next few weeks the witness felt 'strange' at the site. Once driving past with his wife he stopped and got out (feeling an urge to do so). He stared into space for some moments before his frightened wife dragged him back in. Afterwards he took long detours to avoid the area altogether. The timings for the journey on 17 March also had major discrepancies and, whilst he never claimed this, there were grounds to suspect a forty-five minute period of missing time.

Although I kept in touch with the witness for four years and suggested hypnosis he was clearly not happy with the thought. Several anonymous callers had attempted to pressure him into this even before I mentioned it. Who these were or how they concluded that the case was a potential abduction remains unknown. Remember that in 1978 Budd Hopkins had published nothing and the curious aspects of this story were far less obvious to a researcher then than they would be now.

Sadly, we never got a chance to learn the truth. A few months after the experience the unfortunate victim began to feel tired and suffer stomach pains. Cancer of the kidneys was diagnosed. He had successful surgery for this, but shortly afterwards cancer was found in his throat. He had further treatment and surgery but died in early 1982, aged just forty-two. Whether there is any connection between this tragedy and his ordeal is impossible to say. I spoke with him a few weeks before he died and he never once suggested that there was a link. But given the physical effects that were associated with this incident we cannot rule it out.

Ghostly figures such as this feature in other UFO cases. On 12 November 1976 at the Talvera la Real Air Force base near Badajoz on the Spain-Portugal border, two sentries heard an acute whistling noise that was so intense it hurt their ears. Going outside they observed a bright light in the sky and were then met by a third guard who had also seen it. Fearing sabotage they sounded the alarm and were ordered to do a thorough search with one of the base's German Shepherds.

The dog showed no reaction as they proceeded, until a sudden 'whirlwind' struck with very localised blasts of wind. They sent the dog into some bushes where the noises seemed to emerge from and it came staggering back, as if sea-sick and apparently trying to protect its ears from a painful sensation. Then it began to circle them, as it was trained to do whenever it sensed any danger.

Their own senses now twitching the men swivelled around to be confronted by an eerie green glow out of which a misty figure seemed to appear, floating in mid air with legs and other extremities not fully formed. It seemed very large indeed.

One soldier attempted to fire his rifle but felt all the strength drain from his body and began to lose his eyesight. He cried out, 'They'll kill us' as he collapsed onto the floor, conscious but unable to move. His two colleagues did manage to fire, up to fifty rounds, straight into the apparition that was right in front of them. There was a flash of light and like a picture on a TV screen the entity simply disappeared.

The affected soldier later suffered several recurrences of severe head pains and spontaneous loss of vision. He was eventually transferred to a hospital where he was diagnosed as suffering from a 'nervous' disorder without any evident physical cause. He gradually recovered.

However, possibly the oddest part of the story was that despite a thorough investigation (mounted immediately as most of the base heard the shots being fired) not a single bullet was ever traced and no marks were in the wall in front of which the entity had stood.

At another military base, Dakelia in Cyprus, a remarkably similar story was reported to me by a sincere and brave military guard.

He was inside his room at 3 a.m. with his Turkish Wolfhound one night in September 1968 when he also heard a high pitched whine like electric equipment and saw a bizarre figure floating up the stairs glowing bright orange. Its hair was sticking out as if shock full of electricity.

The guard slammed the door but the sound came closer. So he shot the being through the door with his underwater spear gun, an act that indicates his absolute terror. The soldier was found an hour or so later by a relief guard, still shaking on his bed.

This man later suffered muscular paralysis but recovered. The dog was permanently disabled, turning from a fierce guard dog to a terrified and timid creature that hid at the least noise.

Whether there is a connection between the fact that all these cases involve military or research establishments is an interesting question. Is the phantasmagorical nature of entities such as these the result of some sort of technology capable of generating visions? They certainly have that form and have very high energy levels connected with them.

Of course, as usual, in all these cases most people assume that they are extraterrestrial creatures and interpret them accordingly. But perhaps many alien encounters begin as more visionary experiences before the expectations of the witness, the conditioning of society and the belief systems imposed upon them by visiting investigators or the media transform the facts into the more standard extraterrestrial form.

Projections

Are some entities projections akin to modern day holograms?
This may be suggested by a case from Kimba, South Australia.

On 4 February 1973 a nurse and her boyfriend were driving
happily along the monumental trans-continental Eyre Highway
after a night out when they came upon an orange rectangle
beside the road. What seemed to be a very large human figure
loomed dramatically before them, outlined in white, and
standing there silhouetted quite eerily against this mass.

The effect seems to have been remarkably similar to that
portrayed fifteen years later in the hit TV series 'Quantum
Leap'. Here a quantum physicist from the 1990s time-travels
back to the sixties and seventies aided by one of his colleagues
from the future. This helper can only project himself in the
form of a hologram and enters and re-enters space-time
through a doorway against which he stands silhouetted.

At Kimba the courting couple had no such science-fiction
imagery to guide their interpretation. They simply saw this
shape and assumed it was a real entity standing in a doorway of
an otherwise invisible craft. They sped past the horrifying sight
as fast as they could, but did glance back to see that the glowing
figure was now covering the width of the road.

The couple went straight to the police, who were convinced
by their shocked state and tracked down two other vehicles on
the road at the time. Both drivers also saw something similar in
the field that night.

Keith Basterfield of UFO Research Australia, who
investigated the case, pointed out that this highway is notorious
for generating unusual mirage effects, being in places a long flat
stretch with desert and bush to the north and sea to the south.
At times the glow from trains coming down the tracks that run
parallel with the road can be seen up to an hour before they
reach your side from almost 100 miles distant.

However, there must be doubts as to whether such an
explanation can apply at Kimba because this type of entity is far
from unique. An almost identical case occurred on the other
side of the world to a young couple who knew nothing about
this earlier Australian episode.

This second case occurred in a geographically quite different
situation, the foothills of the Pennines at Worrall near
Sheffield, England. At 9 p.m. one night in April 1977 another

courting couple in their car were on a quiet back road here when they observed a bright orange hemisphere behind them. Within this was a silhouetted figure of a very large humanoid that was again outlined in white. The whole thing seemed to be drifting towards them and they drove off at speed, desperate to escape. There was once more another vehicle in the area at the time and the couple's car radio was switched on and exhibited excessive static during the encounter.

There are several other extraordinarily similar reports and all have features in common; such as a very vivid colour (orange or green being most common) and extreme size of the entity which is often a mere outline. Now that we are familiar with holograms, it is intriguing that the same vivid colours are also known to be involved in their production (as dictated by the laser light used to create them).

Are these entity reports the result of some advanced holographic projection rather than an actual visitation? And if so – who are the projectors?

The Humanoids

Devil's Garden sits by the banks of the River Weaver in rural Cheshire. It is an evocative place to fish. You can almost sense the legendary wraith-like bogarts that are said to inhabit the trees when the shadows gather.

For four youths in late January 1978 this was part of the thrill, as was the fact that they were poaching on land where they had no right to be. Alert to any noise or movement in the bushes they pursued their quest on a cool and cloudy night. What the men aged between seventeen and nineteen were not to know was that they were about to become the prey of hunters who were distinctly not of this world.

Jim glanced skyward expecting to see a meteor which had caught his eye, but instead he saw an object that fell from the air in a silent and unremarkable descent. He nudged his friend, Bill, whose father was a local state official and so was more than wary of being mixed up in this daring venture.

'What is it?' he asked.

'I don't know – a satellite maybe?' came the reply.

It was true that just a few days before a Soviet space probe had crashed to earth scattering radioactive debris over the Canadian snows. Luckily nobody was injured, but the newspapers had remarked that there was a great deal of junk floating in orbit and that what goes up eventually comes down. Next time this might not be onto some frozen and uninhabited wasteland or the middle of the sea, it could be somewhere such as the banks of a gently flowing stream rolling through the English countryside.

The four men all watched now as the object (like a silver balloon or egg cup standing upside down) came to rest on a skirt in the grass. Its landing was too controlled. Surely no Russian spacecraft would crash like this.

But if not a terrestrial source, then where did it come from?

They looked at one another as if afraid to voice an answer. A brief glance skyward into the steely cover of the winter's night revealed no stars – but they all knew the stars were up there. Now this thing was down here.

The youths edged closer. Bill was the first to spot a motion coming from around the object's side. There were men in this thing – strange men – and there was no reason to assume that they were friendly.

All four quickly yanked themselves back behind some foliage. They wanted to run and escape from this unexpected nightmare, but they were too afraid to do so. If they were seen in this attempt there was no way of knowing what price they might have to pay.

The men from the silvery dome were small and wore the most peculiar suits, made of something like bacofoil that wrapped them tight as if a second silvery skin. It covered their entire bodies up to their heads and ended in a balaclava helmet. On top of that there was a lamp, not unlike those a miner might wear. From this an eerie sort of glow projected forward, as it did from the base of the craft. It was soft and fuzzy with a purple-pinkish glow. If you looked at it for long enough your eyes began to water.

Now the small group of men were erecting some kind of machine that they had brought from the rear of their craft. It was like a large rectangular climbing frame made of metal bars. It was light – as if composed of aluminium – and they were carrying it without much effort. You could also move it up and down, with the bars swinging sideways so that the whole thing began to resemble a cage ... That thought struck fear into the hearts of the watching poachers.

The strange beings carried the frame across the grass. If they saw their observers they paid no heed to them at all. The strangers' attention seemed focused on two cows that stood by the riverside as similar herds did all over Cheshire that night. These cattle were oblivious to the intruders. One in particular just stood there, neither moving nor mooing. It allowed the silver-clad beings to place the framework around it, to move the bars up and down and sideways and completely hem the animal in.

Still gazing on in astonishment the four teenagers were bemused by what was happening. Were these beings attempting to kidnap the cow? No – rather it seemed as if they used the frame to take measurements. Possibly this was a prelude to capture, but for now they just were studying the mesmerized beast as if it were the first time they had ever witnessed such a creature.

Jim looked at Bill and whispered as softly as he could; 'You know we might be the next!'

Bill agreed. As one, and despite the dangers, the men turned and fled.

They did not get very far before there was a tugging, tingling sensation on their nether regions. Chris, who brought up the rear and was straggling behind, was most aware and most vulnerable. For him it was as if a red hot poker had been pushed down his trousers. It was an excruciating and embarrassing pain. He was, needless to say, quite scared to death.

By now the others had reached a bridge that led to the safety of a road and – they hoped – to sanctuary. Chris, yanking free of the grinding sensation, had hobbled up behind them and was saying very little through panting breath and muffled groans.

None looked behind to see if the beings were still there. None were concerned about the fate of the cow. All were merely grateful to be out of that devilish place and on their way to somewhere which had very earthly welcoming lights and – most of all – other human beings.

This case occurred amidst a wave of entity sightings in northern England in the first few weeks of 1978. The youths, here not named, told their story with great reluctance upon later investigation and insisted that no publicity be given to their identity. They were, of course, mindful of the trespass which they had performed but were also afraid that their amazing tale would simply never be believed.

In the days after this event they developed a red soreness or rash on the lower parts of their bodies. UFO investigators suspect that the purple-pinkish light that they had observed from the alien lamps and the base of the craft was an ultra-violet source and the radiation that may have accompanied it could have led to their physical problems.

This was one of the first occasions where aliens reputedly took a deep interest in cattle. It was not to be the last. Before long investigators would suggest from cases such as this that aliens were surgically removing organs from cattle all over the world and were responsible for the so-called 'mutilations' first noted in the American mid-west during the 1960s. Why were they doing this? What use could they have for organs and blood – which in many cases was found to be drained right away? The clues were to unfold gradually over coming years, but suspicions grew that aliens were performing genetic experiments ... and that – just as Jim had suspected on that January night – after cattle, human beings might be next on an alien shopping list.

The Frodsham cow-napping is yet another remarkable case from within that zone of strangeness south of Warrington where all manner of odd things have been taking place for many years. It is also typical of the humanoid group of aliens of approximately normal size, although usually (as here) slightly smaller, perhaps 5 feet tall.

The activities that they tend to be associated with are often akin to this. In many respects they act like scientists engaged in a research mission and nothing illustrates that better than this incident. It is quite common for them to be relatively uninterested in whoever may be watching them. A commonly used phrase by witnesses is that the humanoids act as if they 'have a job to do'.

PART THREE

Aliens Worldwide

The suspicion by now may be that these alien contacts are a modern psychosis which takes its lead from previous cases and grows with the passage of time and the spread of publicity. Perhaps it is some form of vision or hallucination. Of course, another option must be that there are real alien races of three or four principal types here on earth.

If the latter is to be taken seriously then we should find that this is a worldwide problem, not one confined to western Europe and the USA, as might understandably be presumed from the evidence so far.

We can look at the global scene through a range of cases and see how far this takes us towards answering such questions.

Argentina

The view from within

By April 1957 there had been about forty reported car stop cases, mostly from Europe. They were not well-known outside the small UFO community. But one young man on the road at Pajas Blancas near Cordoba was about to discover that motorcycles were not immune from such puzzling failures.

Riding on a quiet road his engine suddenly died on him. Expecting a mundane fault he got off to investigate the cause, only to find that he was confronted by a huge rounded object that had descended from above and was now hovering just feet in front of him. In terror he leapt into a ditch beside the road.

From this vantage point he saw the object drop lower still until almost on the roadway. Then, with a hiss of air, it ejected a tube or light somewhat like a lift shaft. Within this stood a strange figure.

The entity was described as of normal human height, dressed in a tight-fitting one-piece suit that had a strange sheen as if it were moulded plastic (then much rarer than nowadays of course). All very like ones seen elsewhere. The being had evidently seen the motorcyclist as it came into the ditch and drew him back onto the road, which he did without too much trepidation. The alien had touched the man's forehead and this seemed to have a calming influence. This is another commonly reported feature of these experiences.

It was now obvious that the man was being urged to enter the UFO. This he did by standing beside the entity and finding himself 'floated' up the shaft into a room. Here there were several other figures like the first and also a peculiar illumination that flooded all around and came from no obvious source; although there were some windows that had not been visible whilst he was outside the craft.

This simple view from within seems to have been the entire purpose of the exercise, for after a few moments the awestruck witness was led back down the shaft by his escort, who then gestured farewell by placing a hand onto the man's shoulder. The being then rose back up the tube into the disc, which flew skywards with a bluish-green glow.

The case is quite intriguing because it lacks any of the panache of the contactees or copycat hoaxers from the previous five years which both featured much more exciting plots concerning contact with the entities. The man here claimed no specialness for himself. If this was a hoax it was decidedly dull and has some credibility for that reason.

It was reported immediately, with full conscious memory. Many other people around Cordoba also claim to have seen an object like this on that same day, drifting around the sky and appearing in half a dozen locations as if determined to be spotted. Then it vanished into thin air.

Because of this instant publication we can be certain that this case predates the first abductions, such as the Villas Boas affair in Brazil six months later. It appears to mark a watershed between non-abduction and abduction phases; indeed almost a dry run. It is not difficult to perceive it as a bit like NASA's first Apollo mission in the mid-sixties which began by testing the craft in earth orbit, then flew to the moon but did not land

and eventually went all the way and touched down. This simple story resembles a tentative step towards full scale abduction.

Australia

The lonely sea and sky

Australia has relatively few alien contacts and even fewer abductions, but on the fine evening of Saturday 21 October 1978 it spawned a mystery that remains the talk of the world.

Twenty-year old Frederick Valentich booked out a Cessna 182, call sign Delta Sierra Juliet, from Moorabbin Field, Melbourne. He planned to fly to King Island in the Bass Straits, midway between Tasmania and the mainland. His intention was to get some crayfish for some friends and he had collected $200 (about £100) for that purpose.

The 160 mile flight was just a short hop, but after the Cape Otway lighthouse it would be entirely over open sea. However, it was a nice day and this should not be a real hazard, even though Valentich had little night flying experience.

Oddly, he had booked to leave at 5.35 p.m. and estimated his arrival at 6.40. As this meant he would land on the island whilst it was still partly light there was no surprise when he did not call ahead and ask that the runway lights be on ready for his arrival. But then, as take off time approached, he chose to leave the plane and went for a leisurely meal, returning only in time to take off at 6.19 p.m. as twilight was already taking hold.

Everything went normally until he passed the coast at around 7 p.m. and began his slow descent across the ocean towards King Island. He was now below radar coverage from Melbourne with just radio contact to bridge the twenty minute gap until he approached the island's runway. Their tiny field had no radar system in operation.

Suddenly, at 7.06 the silence was broken when Valentich asked Melbourne if they had other traffic in the area. They said no, but the pilot claimed to have a large aircraft in sight in his vicinity. He then confirmed that he saw four bright 'landing lights' on a dark mass.

The young pilot and Steve Robey (radar controller at Melbourne) engaged in several minutes of conversation. The tape recordings of this was to be significant to aviation authorities and UFO experts alike.

Valentich reported how the large object had flown directly above him at close proximity and great speed, beginning to show strain in his voice for the first time. Robey had made extensive checks and knew that no civil or military aircraft ought to be in the area. Valentich, however, said at one point, 'It's not an aircraft ... it is ...' then trailed off.

A minute later the pilot explained that the object was 'orbiting' directly above him and was metallic in appearance with a green light. At 7.12, six minutes into this terrifying close encounter, the young man uttered fateful words. His engine was 'rough idling' (ie., failing). He confirmed that he was intending to try to make King Island but added in evident awe that the object was still there: 'It *is* hovering and it's *not* an aircraft.' Seconds later the pilot spoke his own call sign and then the radio switch remained depressed for seventeen seconds, the first twelve of which contained strange metal scraping noises, then hiss, then silence.

Neither Valentich nor his Cessna 182 were ever heard from again.

There was, of course, a major search for several days, followed by an intense aviation enquiry, in so far as this was possible without any wreckage to confirm that there had been an accident. Published in May 1982 this effectively concluded that nobody knew what had happened.

There were many theories. That the pilot had inverted his plane in error and was viewing his own reflection in the sea before crashing. That he ran into smugglers using an aircraft trailing a net which snared and felled the Cessna. Or even that he was hit by a falling meteor.

One speculation was that Valentich faked his own disappearance. He was interested in UFOs, had a scrapbook of press cuttings with him on the flight and had seen Spielberg's *Close Encounters* shortly before the tragedy. His plane was filled with four times enough fuel for the trip.

However, the abduction theory was widely accepted in the UFO world, because of the radio conversation and also a big wave of UFO sightings in the Bass Straits area that had occurred immediately prior to this incident. Indeed, two 'contactees' have ever since claimed they have been told Valentich is alive and well on another planet. One has more recently still reported seeing the missing pilot. We may never know the truth.

Belgium

Driven up the wall

Vilvorde is a manufacturing centre a few miles north of Brussels. It has also hosted one of the oddest alien encounters where the entity quite literally was driven up the wall.

It was a cold night in December 1973 and at 2 a.m. a twenty-eight year old married man had to get up to go to the outside toilet in the yard of their home. As he clambered out of the invitingly warm clothes, taking care not to disturb his wife, he took hold of the flashlight kept handy for such purposes and noticed two unusual things.

Fristly, there was a sound like metal scraping on the floor outside. Secondly, instead of the expected total blackness a curious green glow or phosphorescence was coming through the kitchen window.

Intrigued, but not unduly frightened, the man went and parted the curtains, whereupon he was greeted by an unexpected sight. There was a small entity, perhaps 3½ feet tall, wearing a one-piece suit that emitted the strange green glow. On the head was a transparent helmet with a tube leading to a sort of backpack. In fact this was not dissimilar to the beings which had greeted the young man playing hide and seek in that Bolton back yard some fifty years before.

At first the entity was not seen full on, but a glowing red box in the midriff area was also noticed. You will have already appreciated just how common this small detail is within these alien contact stories.

However, the most peculiar feature of this entity was the object that it held out in front of it, sweeping the ground as one might use a metal detector. However, it was larger than that – in fact about the same size and appearance as a household vacuum cleaner or hand held garden mower. It was seemingly sweeping this over the contents of the yard, including some bricks and stones that the witness had left there.

Still without fear, but (as he later saw) oddly not calling to his wife, the witness shone his torch into the garden and seemingly attracted the attention of the entity, for it swivelled around and faced him full on. Now he could see that behind the mask there was a face which had unusually large and rounded eyes and two very pointed ears.

The being seemed to respond to the flashlight signal by raising two of its fingers in a 'V' (for victory) sign. One hopes that it held them the correct way around, otherwise this could have been a most inauspicious start to an extraterrestrial communication!

Now the entity turned back and proceeded to do the most amazing thing. It put one boot against the back wall of the yard, then the other, and without a moment's pause literally walked up the wall sticking out from this at a 90 degree angle and as if magnetized to it. When it got to the top it swivelled around in a smooth arc and vanished over the far side of the wall, at all times keeping the device held out in front.

Surprised, but still not in the least afraid, the witness continued to watch whereupon a glow and a chirping noise came from beyond the wall and an object rose just above this and hovered. It had a small cupola on top of a darker base. The cupola glowed brightly with a blue/greenish hue and inside it was the being. Red sparks were being cast off the junction between the dark lower portion and the brighter top part of the object.

After a couple of minutes the noise increased to a hiss and sparks were thrown off more fiercely. The object rose upwards, accelerating at terrific speed and vanishing into the air in moments, but leaving behind a faintly glowing trail which persisted for a short while.

UFO group SOBEPS conducted an extensive investigation but found no unusual traces in the garden or the land beyond the wall which is owned by a convent. Nobody there saw anything, but from the layout of the building and the land this was not surprising.

In April 1974 the witness was driving late one evening with his wife and cousin near Koningslo on the road to Brussels. They saw a luminous oval object in the sky and the engine and lights of their Ford Escort spluttered and failed. Attempts to restart were unsuccessful. But after a minute the object flew away and the car engine restarted on its own.

This case has the same familiar absurdity we find worldwide.

Brazil

The Alien Alamo

South America is full of alien contact stories and although most countries have their fair share there are undoubtedly more of them in Brazil, from whence the first real abduction was, of course, reported in 1957. Brazil is by far the largest country on the continent, so this is no real surprise.

Ten years before Villas Boas had his sexual encounter, the first traditional alien contact story of the newly born UFO age also occurred here. It came only four weeks after the term 'flying saucer' was invented by the media to describe that sighting by a private pilot in Washington State, USA and was reported and investigated as it happened.

The date was 23 July 1947 and the location Bauru in Sao Paulo. The witness was a surveyor, Jose Higgins, working with a group of men, but the only one who did not run away when the object first came down. They had all heard a high pitched whistle or screech and seen a grey/white disc with a central rim descend from the sky and land in a wooded area.

Left alone, Higgins faced three of the giant entities, estimated as 7 feet tall. They wore one-piece suits and had 'boxes' attached to their backs. Their eyes were huge and round and they seemed to have no evident facial hair.

The beings appeared to try to persuade him to go with them into their craft. One pointed a small hand-held tube at him but nothing happened. He decided that he did not wish to go with them.

One of the entities then drew some marks into the ground with a stick that it picked up. These were in the form of eight holes, as if trying to draw a picture of a solar system or star map. The central one was the biggest (as if it were a sun) and the entity pointed at it and said the word 'Alamo'. Then it pointed to the seventh one and seemed to indicate this was their home, saying the word 'Orque'. However, even this level of friendliness (which Higgins felt clearly) did not entice him to enter the machine.

He noticed that the beings seemed unable to cope with bright sunlight and stayed in the shade as much as possible. It has since been pointed out by interested biologists that in nature the presence of very large eyes suggests that environmental light levels are low and so might here infer visitors from a world where sunlight is much dimmer than on earth. As such they would have real difficulty coping with bright conditions of a sunny day on this planet, which might tie in with the fact that 90 per cent of alien contact cases appear to be nocturnal.

Unaware of any of this at the time, Higgins nonetheless says he used the very obvious fact of their phobia to keep out of reach of the entities, who seemed none too concerned that he did. In fact, they kept picking up big rocks and throwing them about as if playing a game!

After about half an hour the beings went into the object, which then took off into the air again making the screeching whistle.

Once more you see that the larger entities, as elsewhere in the world, here display mild curiosity and scientific endeavour but draw back from using the kind of violence noted often in other circumstances. Indeed, in a not dissimilar situation just three weeks later the small beings at Villa Santina, Italy, used considerable force when they were confronted by a prospecting geologist.

Canada

Too hot to handle

Canada does have alien encounters, but these are much less common than in the USA. Yet one outstanding case offers two vital things – a long close-up inspection by the witness of a landed object and major physical evidence. It has been deeply researched by Chris Rutkowski.

The incident occurred at Falcon Lake, a beautiful little town surrounded by hundreds of small lakes and wild country. This lies just off the Trans-Canada Highway from Winnipeg to Thunder Bay and just into the state of Manitoba. It was 20 May 1967 and the witness was fifty-one year old Stephen Michalak, a family man and mechanic, enjoying a few days amateur prospecting in the rich quartz mineral deposits of the area.

Just after noon in a marshy area a mile from the road, Michalak heard geese and, momentarily startled, looked up to see two oval craft dropping from the sky and glowing bright red. One of these stopped, hovered a while and then flew off, dulling to a grey colour as it did so. But the second came down and hovered very low above the ground.

Michalak, who rapidly assumed that he was witnessing new military aircraft, probably from the USA, watched intently as the object seemed to 'cool' from red hot, to a glowing metal colour. He was wearing welding goggles to protect his eyes from chips of rock. This may have been very fortunate, for a bright purple light was oozing from slits in the top of the machine. This seems to have been ultra-violet light, because it hurt the eyes unprotected by filters covering the goggles.

The prospector sat on a rock sketching the object in detail, noting as he did so the waves of heat coming from it and the odd smell like sulphur that wafted over from its direction. Then a door seemed to open and he decided to go closer. He heard voices coming from inside, affirming his interpretation. So convinced was he that the object was an American test aircraft that he strolled up and popped his head through the door!

Michalak recalls saying, 'OK, Yankee boys, having trouble? Come on out and we'll see what we can do about it.'

There was no reply and the voices stopped. So he tried several other languages that he knew, including Russian, French, German and Italian. There was still no reply. Inside he saw only a series of blinking lights on panels of equipment but the glare was too strong and hurt his eyes. He had to flip down the filter on his goggles.

Stepping back, a bit disappointed, he then saw the panel seal shut and could inspect the surface closely. It was very smooth without joints and was so highly polished it resembled glass, reflecting so strongly that rainbow-coloured spectra were created. Michalak also now noticed that his glove had melted where it had touched the surface and his hat, which must have accidentally brushed against it, was also burnt slightly.

As he was examining this the side of the object seemed to rotate and rise a little. A grill-like vent was now beside him and a blast of hot air shot from this, instantly setting ablaze his shirt and vest. He tore these off admist great pain, causing a small bush fire where they fell. The next thing he knew the object was climbing away skywards with a blast of compressed air, filling his nostrils with both the sulphurous odour and also a smell like burnt electrical wiring.

Staggering back to the rock he found his compass rotating wildly for a few moments and also felt nauseous and had a pounding headache. He decided to abandon prospecting and seek help. It took him a good while to get to the highway, being sick at several points and having to rest as he felt very weak. Eventually Michalak did reach the road and tried to flag down a passing Royal Canadian Police car. He explained what had happened but the officer said he had 'other duties to perform' and drove off.

The witness got back to his motel in Falcon Lake about 4 p.m. but did not go inside for a while, afraid he was 'contaminated' because he was covered in a bad smell. His family confirm this. After asking directions to the nearest doctor he learnt that this was at Kenora, across the state line into Ontario and 45 miles east. So instead he waited for the first bus back to Winnipeg, phoned home and told his wife he'd had a slight accident but not to worry. His older son was asked to collect him from the bus stop when it reached the city at 10.15. Upon seeing his father's condition the young man drove him immediately to Misericordia Hospital.

At the hospital Michalak told the examining doctor that he had been burnt by exhaust from an aircraft and did not elaborate. The burns, formed into a clear checkerboard pattern, were photographed and treated and Michalak was then released. Next day he called the local paper to report the incident, claiming he felt it was his 'duty' to do so.

On 22 May the witness was visited by his own doctor, who noted that the burns were second degree and minor; although twenty years later in 1987 Rutkowski reports the skin was still affected. Medication was given and then on 23 May Michalak had gone to see a radiation specialist but was diagnosed as suffering from chemical burns that were heat induced, not from radiation. The nausea and tiredness were now subsiding but the witness claims he ate poorly for some time and lost a lot of weight. The only slight anomaly was that two blood counts taken by a nuclear research establishment in late May suggested a 10 per cent drop in blood lymphocytes but on each occasion coupled with normal platelet readings which tends to mitigate against suggestions of radiation poisoning.

In August 1968, after various unsubstantiated accusations (eg., that he had burnt himself building homemade rockets or fallen in a drunken state onto a barbecue) he checked in at his own considerable expense to the famed Mayo Clinic in the USA. Despite having documentary proof that he was there, as alleged, they later denied he had ever attended and sent no results. Following this denial Michalak sent a copy of his discharge papers and the clinic immediately affirmed they had seen him, but found only slight hyperventilation and no major physical problems. Psychiatric tests also carried out at Michalak's insistence found no evidence for hallucinations, delusions or emotional disorders.

There were several peculiarities about the investigation of the site. Michalak took three attempts to find it; although he gave reasonable excuses for this. Soil samples taken there allegedly found sufficiently high levels of radium for the Department of Health and Welfare to consider closing off the immediate area to all visitors. However, subsequent samples were taken and only a tiny area was irradiated. Elsewhere there was only the background levels created by local uranium. So the region was not sealed off.

This case remains contentious but most people who have met Michalak are convinced by his sincerity.

Russia

Giants in the park

On 9 October 1989 I faced a most unusual but welcome event. I had to appear live on the national ITN news to discuss 'the big one'; that UFO case we had always thought would never happen. The incident that finally would prove to the world the reality of alien contact.

In fact, this was, of course, an exaggeration. But it was not one made by UFOlogists. They had been typically cautious on the matter. The rush to judgement came from extraordinary sources, such as the prestigious newspaper offices of the *Washington Post* and *New York Times* and equivalents. *The Times* even contemplated this as being 'the story of the century' and cautioned against readers being too sceptical. Yet far more probative cases than this one are happening all of the time right on their doorsteps and are constantly being ignored or ridiculed.

What led to such a dramatic turnabout? The answer was simple. The alien contact in question was being confirmed by the normally staid Soviet press agency TASS and, as a spokesman told a BBC TV newscast, looking personally affronted that such a suggestion had ever been made, the case was 100 per cent genuine because 'TASS *never* jokes!'

So what case broke the decades of silence and state insistence that UFOs were capitalist fairytales? Sadly you would not have got the facts from the very brief western press blitz about this 'story of the century'. It took UFOlogists weeks of hard work to get hold of those, by which point, of course, the media had long since lost interest.

It transpired that there was an impressive case amidst a whole wave of events between 21 September and 28 October 1989. These mainly focused on the Western Park area of Voronezh, an industrial city, similar in size to Manchester, and some 200 miles south of Moscow in what is now Russia. The location was appropriately named, for the dying Soviet Union was getting its first real taste of western style UFOlogy and its attendant hype care of this burst of close encounters.

Many of the sightings were made by children playing in the park. Indeed, one Soviet TV network soon gave up on the story because they failed to find adults willing to go on record. However, one or two were eventually persuaded to talk, including a military officer who chanced to be in the area but had deliberately kept quiet about what he saw. It has to be realized that adults probably had much experience of the Communist regime and its repression, so, unlike children, they felt inhibited about relating things that for years they had been told were anti-state.

Nevertheless, there seems little doubt that some of the witnesses were telling the truth as they saw it and Viktor Atlasov, city mayor, professed his faith in their testimony after internal criminal department investigations by Colonel Militia Lyudmilla Makarova.

By the time of the main event there had been several reports of lights and entities, described as both humanoids and robots. These varied considerably from case to case. Eventually as many as 300 people gathered in the park in typical 'skywatch' looking for the red light that was often witnessed and soon nicknamed 'the saucer'.

On 27 September, around 6.30 p.m., a crowd of onlookers, some people going home from work and at a nearby bus-stop and the much more talkative children, who were aged thirteen to sixteen and engaged in a game of football, all spotted a 'pink haze' in the sky. This was described as looking like a bonfire through mist. It circled the park as more and more people began to watch it.

Suddenly, in a scene intriguingly reminiscent of that in Rendlesham Forest, Suffolk, nine years earlier, or, indeed, of the encounter at Imjarvi in Finland even earlier than that, a silvery sphere exploded out of the mist in a flash of light and descended towards the poplar trees.

As the thing came down, witnesses report how the trees bent beneath the pressure and a door opened in the side of what was now seen to be a banana-shaped object. A strange and very tall humanoid (9 or 10 feet is estimated) looked out, as if inspecting the scene below. Then the door closed and the object pushed further down into the tree until it was as low as it could get towards the ground and the door opened once again. Now several beings got out and scrambled down the trunk (or according to some sources a ladder that was deployed) into the park.

There are conflicting accounts as to how many were seen or whether a 'metal robot' appeared (some say this was one child's confabulation). Some also said the beings had a third eye or light atop their head.

Further stories associated with the case are hard to pin down and are bizarre even by the peculiarities we associate with alien contact.

For example, one was that a being fired a yellow pistol at a man walking towards the bus stop who had stopped to stare at the entities. A beam emerged and the man vanished, returning only after the UFO had left, still in mid stride, walking on as if he had seen nothing at all.

Or the 'fact' that two entities strode purposefully towards an electricity pylon and one attempted to climb it, catching fire and literally burning into a frazzle of nothingness!

It seems that this is partly due to the intermixing of earlier landings (the pylon incident in the park was on 23 September and only a couple of children were witnesses). Also it was through the fact that the story spread around the romantically named 'school 33' where most of the teenage witnesses were based. No doubt a few must have later invented things so as not to be left out or to gain attention from their friends.

What is clear is that when the object came down over the tree, some legs extended out and touched the ground. These left imprints which were studied by several scientists, notably Dr Henry Silanov, a local geologist who has since kindly confirmed his part in the affair by letter. The military police also looked at these and the consensus view was that an object weighing 11 tons was responsible.

No fewer than seventeen soil samples were taken from the site and studied at the nuclear physics department of Voronezh

University. Between two to three times the normal background gamma radiation count was found, but only inside the landing zone and at maximum within the indentations. These are abnormal but not a threat to health.

Oddly on 28 October a spokesman for the university retracted these claims and suggested that the levels were probably just fall-out from the Chernobyl nuclear explosion in 1986. However, what is fascinating is that this precise level of radiation and its maximization within the indentations are both exactly what was found by USAF investigators in Rendlesham Forest, England after the intriguingly similar encounter there in December 1980. That was six years *before* the Chernobyl accident.

United Kingdom

So sad to see them go

Reactions to a close encounter are fascinating because they can be so different. Someone may respond with terror, others in surprising ways.

The experience of Jenny, an exceptionally intelligent, rational and lucid care assistant from West Yorkshire had a great effect on Roy Sandbach and me when we investigated her sighting. She is a perfect example of a sincere witness and shows why the evidence for this phenomenon can be powerfully persuasive to those who go out and seek it.

At the time of her encounter, November 1978, she lived in a hill village called Walsden, two miles from Todmorden, West Yorkshire. That town may well lay claim to the UFO abduction capital of Europe as so many impressive alien contacts have occurred in its rural surroundings. Indeed, two years to the day after Jenny's encounter began with the sighting of some lights, and when her story had been published nowhere, the Walsden village bobby was abducted from his patrol car on the Burnley Road in a case that is famous in the UFO world.

Jenny's encounter may be as important. Her background is surprisingly common in witnesses to the alien contact; although most researchers, let alone abductees, are unaware of this fact.

For example, between the ages of five and eight she reports how strange balls of light about the size of a small basketball would enter her bedroom and float around. As soon as she called her parents, the 'fire' vanished. Witnesses who describe these often say they felt good about the visitations and would even play with them. They seem to act as gentle introductions towards subsequent encounters and I call them 'psychic toys', because they do function rather like toys in a child's physical development. It is as if they help the future abductee grow into an ability to shift states of consciousness.

Paranormal experiences are rife throughout later childhood and early adulthood of these people. With Jenny they included frequent lucid dreams (where she was able to control her dream state consciously whilst still dreaming), false awakenings (where she believed that she was awake only to discover she was still dreaming) and out of body experiences, where she claimed to travel mentally to other places and later verify the incidents that occurred there with those she 'saw'. Premonitions and apparitions are also common and Jenny had examples of these as well.

Her close encounter itself straddled that illusionary border between physical reality and altered state of consciousness. She had been horse riding and was returning home with her dog down the hillsides when something caused the animal to stop frolicking and, in a way it never did before or since, look up at the sky. Jenny followed its gaze and saw an object that she admits she would have otherwise walked right underneath.

It was a lens shape with a neon blue body and windows or portholes on the edge. Surrounding it was a silver/green mist or fog out of which it just seemed to emerge. Jenny says that she was transfixed by this majestic silence and was given an absolutely ecstatic feeling. She felt that everything else was drained from her consciousness and it was as if she and the alien presence were, as she put it, 'joined at the soul'. Whilst not a deeply religious person she said that the sense of oneness was akin to how she imagined meeting God might be.

After the experience, Jenny's rational self kicked in and she constantly questioned why others did not see this thing. The sight was so spectacular half of the people in the region should have done. Yet it was as if only she (and her dog) had been singled out for contact. Another anomaly she spotted was the brilliance of the glow and its proximity to the ground but the fact that it failed to illuminate the hillside. This seemed physically impossible but it was happening.

As she stood in what Whitley Strieber perceptively named a

decade later a sort of 'communion' with the phenomenon she
sensed an alien voice tickling her mind during the altered state
of consciousness she knew that she must have been in. The
voice said plainly 'do not be afraid', but she expects that
anybody who had been with her at the time might not have
heard it. Instantly, upon 'sensing' this voice, she went from
utter terror to 'calm, peace and loving security'.

Jenny said that at this point; 'I swear that had something got
out of the thing and said 'come with me' I would have followed
like a lamb.' She now knows that the effect on her was
hypnotic. The alien phenomenon was literally luring her into a
trap from which not only could she not escape but did not want
to escape.

Her next recollection was that time and space had become
meaningless. She was in what we call an 'Oz Factor' union with
the intelligence and felt it sift through her mind sampling her
lifetime's experiences.

Then, suddenly, she knew that the object was about to leave
and she felt terrible sadness. Jenny reports (and is by no means
alone in expressing similar sentiments), 'I pleaded with them to
stay. But I knew it had to go. I was told that I was not harmed,
would not be harmed and would be protected.' Then it split in
two and, trailing a shower of sparks, shot 'like stones from a
catapult' across the sky.

Jenny is not afraid to report that she stood on the moors
staring into the empty sky, tears streaming down her face at the
combined rapture and misery of the indescribable event. Such a
response, which she knew nobody could possibly understand
and which she herself struggled to accept, was what provided
the greatest barrier towards telling others. The experience itself
was less important than the effect it had on her.

The woman at interview tried desperately to put the
encounter into terms others could comprehend. 'I was divorced
from myself during its presence. It drained me of all my
essence. I know this sounds terribly subjective but it was as if I
were a computer terminal ... It gets so frustrating visualizing
this and not being able to put it into words.'

Jenny suggested that you should imagine walking across the
hills and finding the QE II liner suspended in the sky. You rub
your eyes, blink, but it is still there. Then it just disappears.
Afterwards you know without a moment's doubt that it was
really there but you also know that nobody else in the world

could possibly believe you if you tried to tell them. The feeling
of helplessness this creates is far worse than the encounter
itself, she explains in a way that I found moving and utterly
convincing.

There seems to be a deeper memory behind the case, but
Jenny decided not to use hypnosis to try retrieval, after
thinking long and hard.

She says this '... hovers on the border of my memory ... It is
teasing me at the edge of understanding. I believe that one day
I shall know the truth about all this when they are ready. But
that time is not now.'

These are the exact sentiments that witnesses of alien contact
are reporting all over the world in a way that is frighteningly
identical. Anyone who takes the trouble to talk to several
people like Jenny soon becomes persuaded that whatever is
happening, and we do not know what, this is a very real and
deeply significant phenomenon.

As for what form it takes – reality, visionary, both or neither
– it is clear that there is far more to it than straightforward
extraterrestrial Neil Armstrongs landing in Venusian space
shuttles and saying 'take me to your leader'. Cases such as
Jenny's probe closer to the raw essence of these encounters
because she strips bare the emotion and the life-changing
response. Fourteen years later the contact actually 'haunts' her
life. She knows she will never escape from it.

It is worth noting that there is another form of strange
phenomenon that shares eerily similar features to the alien
contact. But it is being investigated by a completely different
group of researchers, doctors and psychologists, mostly
unaware of the links. In both sets of data the witness has a
conditioning track record of strange phenomena, has far above
average visual creativity, enters an altered state of consciousness at the onset of the encounter, sees a brilliant light with
magical or mystical properties, enters into communion, has
contact with a vastly superior intelligence, is told that they must
return even though they wish to enter the wondrous light and
share its oneness, often report being scanned or probed with
life reviews and are sent back with a feeling that there is more
buried deep inside them to be triggered at a later date. These
people often return to normal consciousness forever altered by
their experience and with deep sadness that it has ended.

The phenomenon with such remarkable parallels has been

researched by science during almost exactly the same time scale as the abduction. They call it the NDE – or Near Death Experience – and is usually interpreted as a glimpse of the afterlife or a realm of consciousness 'beyond' life.

NDE specialist Dr Kenneth Ring has chanced upon the startling patterns that a few UFOlogists have been pointing to for a decade. We may finally begin to seek what links these two incredible experiences.

United States

An altered reality

David Stephens, aged twenty-one, and his eighteen year old friend, both worked on nightshifts at local factories and shared a trailer home at Norway in Maine. So it was not unusual to find them up and about listening to music at 3 a.m. on 27 October 1975. But this time their decision was to have a profound effect on their lives.

They were first alerted by a noise like an explosion and went outside into the woods to check, but nothing was visible. So, on the spur of the moment, they set off in their car to drive around the lake near Oxford. However, the driver found himself led on impulse down a back road unable to halt this progress.

About a mile south of Oxford the two men saw a pair of white headlights which at first they took to be a truck stopped on the road ahead. They slowed down but the lights rose up into the air. Thinking now it was a helicopter they wound down the windows and switched off the engine for a better view. A mass of multi-coloured lights surrounded the silent object which had now begun to chase them!

Switching the car back on, the two men set off, but then there was a sudden blink in reality. Their next conscious memory was of being about a mile away with the car on the wrong side of the road and the doors unlocked. The two men stared at one another mystified.

They drove off but 'on impulse' headed towards Tripp Pond, where the car engine and radio failed. Here they were trapped on this remote road for an hour and a half with strange lights moving above them. Then a peculiar fog closed in on the car. Finally it disappeared and at 6.30 a.m. they were able to start the engine and drive home, determined to say nothing of their adventure.

However, upon arrival home both men felt lightheaded, had sore eyes and were disorientated. Their hands lacked coordination, they could hardly stand up and found it difficult even to talk coherently. During the encounter and its aftermath they had severe distortions of reality with mundane things taking on extraordinary proportions. They saw 'snow' falling when no snow was present, black cubes floating around the living-room which others told them were not there. There is even some reason to suggest that a 'mother ship' they believe was present throughout their encounter was in fact simply the moon, grossly misperceived.

About forty hours after the sighting when investigators first visited the men they were still acting like this, interpreting what were very obviously stars as strange UFOs. This disorientation gradually subsided.

Whilst this might seem a significant detraction from their story it is in fact a common aftermath, as if witnesses find it extremely difficult to shift their consciousness back to the 'real world' after experiencing the bizarre reality of the close encounter. Tricksters are hardly likely to damage their own credibility so readily by admitting such things.

Between December 1975 and March 1976 several hypnosis sessions were conducted by Dr Herbert Hopkins. Only David Stephens was regressed as his friend was too upset and, in fact, moved 2,000 miles away soon after the sighting wanting to 'forget the whole thing'.

During the hypnosis David recounted an experience where his friend was left in the car and he was floated into a strange room. Here he encountered beings about 4½ feet tall with heads shaped like lamps and large slanted eyes. They wore loose garments 'like a sheet' and conversed mentally with him. They showed him a table in a room with equipment and he understood they wanted him to lie on this, but he resisted vigorously. Then, suddenly, in the next instant he got onto the table without any further questioning. He still does not know why.

A fairly standard medical examination followed, in which his clothes were removed and blood and hair samples were extracted. He felt no pain during this time. David was told that they would see him again in the future and information was implanted into his mind which made him very upset when he tried to remember. He explains that he made a 'promise' and that 'this data will be buried in his subconscious for the moment'.

This case was not well-known, even in UFO circles, when five years later police officer Alan Godfrey was abducted from his patrol car under two miles from the site of Jenny's 1978 experience as we have just reviewed. Under hypnosis the police officer revealed details that were remarkably similar to those described by David Stephens, even though it seems very unlikely the British bobby knew about the case 3000 miles away.

The 1980 Todmorden abduction involved entities 'the size of a five year old lad' with heads shaped 'like a lamp'. A taller human-like being was in control. He wore a garment 'like a white sheet'. The police man was led towards a table or bed, just as David Stephens had been. This is how the officer described what happened next. He said the entities 'want me to get on [the table]' and when asked by the psychiatrist if he intended to do so, replied 'not bloody likely!' But then, in the very next sentence he reported getting onto it.

There were more patterns – similarities in the medical examination, promise of a return visit, information planted into his mind which pained him when he tried to recall it. The parallels are striking.

It is this kind of thread weaving cases together around the world that seems to insist that we take this matter very seriously. Whatever its cause it seems to be disturbingly consistent.

Part Three: Summary

I could continue with stories from all around the world and we would fill several volumes and still not exhaust the supply.

In Japan hypnotic regression is revealing hidden abductions just as it is in the USA and Britain and the details are all too familiar.

On the Island of Reunion in the Indian Ocean there have been a spate of landings where entities wearing 'Michelin Man' suits have appeared.

In Zimbabwe, Africa, research by Cynthia Hind is uncovering many cases just like those appearing elsewhere, usually involving young women who are abducted from their bedrooms.

Even in Lon Xi, China, we have a growing number of cases escaping the Communist repression, such as the silver-suited small entity seen beside a blue glow that was astride a road.

However, there are notable exceptions. The vast continent of India and Pakistan has, so far as we know, virtually no alien contact cases. This may simply be an omission due to lack of researchers looking for them but one would expect, given the huge population of the sub-continent, that there should have been enough examples of a global phenomenon to ensure that we had a healthy record. This gap is intriguing and important.

Indeed, generally speaking, the abduction is a white Caucasian experience. I strongly emphasize that this is not meant as a racist remark. Nor is it absolutely true. A classic case from Papua, New Guinea, for example, involved a missionary, Father Gill, with whom I had the pleasure of spreaking, and a whole host of local natives who observed a UFO and entities suspended over their villages, and Cynthia Hind has found cases from native Africans, where they are usually interpreted as visits from ancestral spirits.

However, these cases are definitely much rarer than we would expect, even in countries such as the USA where there is a very healthy inter-racial culture.

Another fascinating puzzle is why the evidence points in two different directions when it comes to the types of entity seen.

Whilst there is undoubtedly a level of comparison between cases that looks to be far beyond chance expectation, particularly given the wide extent of human imagination (in science-fiction for example) there is nevertheless a degree of cultural stereotyping. This was especially the case in the first two or three decades of reports; although since about 1980 cases around the world have rather standardized into a few familiar types.

In the earlier records you see patterns such as these:

South America – small, swarthy dwarves who were fairly aggressive.
North America – small, egg-head scientists, often called 'greys' because of their skin colour.
Europe – taller, blond haired, blue eyed 'Norse god' type entities with a paranormal bag of tricks (eg., walking through walls) and rather friendlier disposition.

There are other trends, but even these are enough to illustrate a real problem. Why should the earth be divided like this if we really are being visited (as UFOlogists claim) by a range of alien races? Are they metaphorically saying you can have America, we'll take Europe?

Is it also important that there is a symbiosis between alien type and the culture of the civilization (eg., clever, egocentric scientists in the USA, reserved and diffident mystics in Europe)?

And, odder still, why have the cases evened out as time has gone by, with the rest of the world seeming to gradually adopt the American standard alien (the grey) to what is now a much greater extent? Is it relevant that American reports of this entity type are the ones that have had by far the most publicity and influence on people around the world who have come into contact with alien contact literature, generating far more cases and books on the subject than any other country?

Questions such as these must be looked at by any researcher trying to resolve the phenomenon of alien contact. Sadly all too many are ignoring the consequences.

PART FOUR

An Alien Identikit

A brief time-out now will let us sketch identikit portraits of six main types of alien that emerge from the data. I exclude near normal looking entities, often with beards, who represent around 10 per cent of the data.

I should stress this is not a claim that any of these beings *really* exist, merely a reflection of the evidence that is reported. We now have about 4000 well researched alien contact cases on record from around the world. These (seven) types account for about 92 per cent of all such sightings.

1 The Apparition

Rare, representing only about 4 per cent of cases, this is typified by examples such as the Risley, Cheshire, Talavera, Spain and Dakeelia, Cyprus reports, where the entity resembles a phantom or projection. Occasionally appears inside buildings, often walking through walls like a ghost.

Most events occur on open roads and appear and disappear suddenly in the form of a hologram or image (e.g., the Eyre Highway case from South Australia). The ability to pass through solid objects is widely described (e.g., the atomic plant security fence at Risley).

Hardly ever (if at all) do these involve abductions into a strange object but frequently they are associated with strong physical energies and ill-effects on witnesses and animals. There is a suspicion that ionizing radiation is emitted during these encounters.

Such cases resemble animate creatures from another world far less than any of the other alien types and may well be entirely different from them, requiring a unique solution.

Of significance is that most do not involve the presence of any real UFO in association with the figure – in all four cases (from various parts of the world) that are discussed above.

2   The Robot

Robotic creatures are common in science-fiction but rare in the actual records (about 5 per cent of cases). They are hardly ever seen on their own and in nearly all cases found in the presence of other entities, usually either the greys or the Nordic humanoids.

They seem to have the function of menials or servants and on more than one occasion terms such as 'retrieval device' have been used to describe them (according to what witnesses believe they were told).

They are quite common in abduction situations assisting with medical examinations. In the Alan Godfrey, Todmorden case, robots were supervised by a normal sized entity with a beard. In the Telford, Shropshire abduction they were associated with study of the witness and alongside both Nordics and greys in the same UFO.

On a few occasions robotic creatures have been seen outside UFOs as if seeking 'samples' to take back into the object, without the real occupants therefore ever appearing beyond the confines of the craft.

In close proximity to a witness they are said to be smooth and shiny but there is little evidence that they are metallic in construction, or indeed akin to robots as we know them. Shape and size varies considerably from small to gigantic and they have been both silent and noisy. Only their purpose seems to be consistent.

3   The Goblin

Grotesque creatures that resemble goblins and trolls from the folklore of many nations are surprisingly reported in about 7 per cent of cases.

They seem to pop up almost anywhere and are as frequent now as they were in the past, with cases such as a frightening house siege in Kentucky, USA, 1955, the flying animal snatchers of Puerto Rico in the 1970s and the 1987 entity photographed on Ilkley Moor in England (See page 118).

Although they are sometimes seen in association with UFOs they are only infrequently connected with abductions and quite often appear without a 'ship' at all. They seem to blend physical reality with a magical quality (eg., one minute they may be photographed and another a shot might pass straight through as if nothing was there).

Their actions seem frequently rather mischievious or even aggressive, thus emulating the traditions of the goblin from our folk heritage. In many senses these reports merely seem to be a space-age update on entities that legend says have long dwelt in a parallel universe described by the mythology of many nations.

There is an interesting tendency to find that locations where such creatures are seen have a centuries old track-record of mysterious apparitions and local names may even record that by referring to 'devil' places ascribed because of these supernatural goings on.

This suggests to some researchers that the goblins might not be alien visitors at all, but a race of paraphysical entities which co-exist with us and who enjoy play-acting in the guise of aliens as part of their inherent naughtiness. John Keel uses the term 'ultraterrestrials' and FW Holiday designed the concept of the 'Goblin Universe' to locate these beings. It is an idea which the evidence supports quite well.

Equally the thousands of years of intense belief in these entities might have produced a vivid thought imprint on the biosphere of the earth which allows them to occasionally be 'seen' by visually creative people, an idea supported by some new wave researchers.

4   The Dwarf

These creatures have many attributes of the goblin and might even be a variation on the same theme. The main distinguishing features are that the goblin has very prominent ears and often a greenish cast (one of the origins of the term little green man) but the dwarf seems to be swarthy and covered in hair.

About 5 per cent of sightings involve this type of entity and they were particularly common in South America during the early 1950s; although there were some reports in Europe (especially France) up until about 1954. Since then they have become very rare.

One of the few modern cases is the Aveley abduction from Essex, England, in October 1974, where the main occupants of the UFO were Nordics but the medical examination was in the hands of several small, ugly creatures that are not unlike the hairy dwarves of twenty years before. In this case they appeared to be biological robots (or androids) and more than one witness who has seen them has been told that they are genetically created semi-intelligent animals bred to do routine tasks.

They are certainly often said to be animalistic in nature, tending towards physical aggression and assault. Their direct association with UFOs is more evident than with the goblins but they rarely seem to be in control of things.

Certainly it is difficult to ignore the parallels with the dwarves of folklore, but as there is so little data from the past forty years it is unwise to draw too many conclusions.

In the 1990s there are hints (mostly in a few extreme US cases) of a new type of animalistic entity often said to have reptilian skin. The impact of this form of alien in the TV drama 'V' and the three popular fiction movies in the *Alien* series seems too coincidental to ignore as a source for this imagery. Whilst some American UFOlogists are taking the existence of reptilian entities very seriously, I think the jury must still be out on the literal reality of such beings.

5   The Greys

If you were to base any conclusion on the sheer number of alien reports the greys (or 'grays' in their native land – the USA) would win hands down. About 37 per cent of all cases seem to describe them, but that percentage post 1980 rises to well above 50 per cent, because they are utterly dominant in the records of the 1980s and 1990s.

The fact that several highly successful books, films and TV mini-series based on 1980s sightings of the greys from the USA have stamped this vision on much of the world surely cannot be irrelevant to this situation. Even respected and committed believers in the reality of alien visitors, such as Jerome Clark, are asking why there is no real sign of grey domination of the literature before the onset of the almost maniacal quest for abductions by the UFO community since the 1960s. Whereas today, amidst all that, greys do indeed swamp the records.

The answer to this question may well help decide whether alien contacts are physically real events or visionary phenomena. Visions would inevitably rely to some extent on prevailing cultural trends, but why should real extraterrestrials?

The features of the grey are known in more detail than any other entity type because we have so many hundreds of examples. They are undoubtedly consistent to an astonishing degree.

Typically they are small, 3½ to 4½ feet being the most common. The skins are said to be white or grey (hence the name) and hairless. Noses and mouths are nondescript, certainly in comparison with the eyes, which powerfully dominate the egg-shaped head. These are extremely large and round, often dark (even black) and at times close-up have been likened to that of an insect. Indeed, the rather spindly nature of the alien frame, with the head perched rather teeteringly on the body, has also been likened to an insect on various occasions.

There are no obvious greys prior to about 1957; although some earlier cases (eg., Villa Santina in 1947) do come close. The form so familiar today has almost exclusively emerged from hypnotic regression during the last twenty years but today we find greys reported without hypnosis as often as those cases stimulated by artificial means.

Undoubtedly the greys are the kings of the abduction and the original medical examiners, both almost a prerequisite of encounters with them. They are said to be engaged in genetic experiments and to treat their abductees rather as we might handle a rat in a laboratory, somewhat indifferently, not seeming to deliberately hurt them but with their own purpose (whatever that be) plainly superior to the welfare of the human victim. Many women in the USA are beginning to allege that they have been gynaecologically manipulated by these entities and some even believe they have had alien/human hybrid foetuses extracted from their womb during an abduction.

In 1970 there were few abductions and at least as many alien contacts were reported without abduction. Whilst greys were seen, they were no more common than various other types.

By 1980, and in particular in the USA, both abductions and sightings of greys were far more prevalent. In the rest of the world a few abductions and greys were beginning to be reported but these were still fewer in number than more simple alien contacts with other entity types.

Finally, by 1990, much of the world was in the grip of an epidemic of abductions and sightings of the greys. In the USA almost nothing else was alleged, with non-abduction alien contacts and sightings of non-grey alien types negligible in numbers. The rest of the world, whilst still not dominated in the same way, was rapidly catching up. This has led to the prediction that by the year 2000 there would be virtually nothing in the records other than abduction by greys universally reported.

Unless, of course, things in this fluctuating subject change again.

6   The Nordics

In the 1950s contactees usually met friendly, relatively human-looking aliens. However, the presence of long, blond hair and blue eyes became quite common aspects. Such features on what were often tall (ie., 6 feet) entities began to dominate the early alien contacts that came as a sequel to the contactee invasion.

This pattern was particularly noticeable in Europe, where the similarity of the beings to the Nordic or Scandinavian race was the source of their name. Throughout the 1950s, 1960s and 1970s alien contacts in countries such as Britain were full of Nordics and they did appear elsewhere, including the USA, before greys became all conquering.

Aside from their height and rather beautiful appearance the Nordics have cat-like, slanting eyes and also differ in that they tend to be more passive observers, rather than interfering meddlers in human affairs. When met and conversed with they seem to be friendlier and generally sympathetic in outlook. On more than one occasion they appeared to be aware of the existence of the greys, warning witnesses that another race of aliens were on earth and that these were not quite so concerned about human welfare as the Nordics themselves claimed to be.

The Nordics seemed keen to spread a contactee message in a rather less overt way, warning witnesses about the abuse of nuclear energy and ecological matters on a one-to-one basis, often by showing vivid imagery. There are even some examples of scientific knowledge being conveyed and they are rather more willing to share information with a witness, even if on the whole this was difficult to understand.

Overall the records show that about 24 per cent of cases involve the Nordics but they have gone through a lingering disppearance from the 1960s onward. At first they began to wear silver suits, as the greys commonly did, so the blond hair and facial features were reported less often. At times it was difficult to tell whether reports really were of the Nordics. However, they were still being seen into the 1980s, particularly outside the USA and especially in Europe although by the 1990s their demise has reached alarming proportions.

Prior to the 1980s, the Nordics were as dominant in the records outside the USA as the greys were within the alien contacts from America.

Nordics have certainly been involved in abductions, but this seems to be less essential to the encounter than it is with the greys. Their appearances together are about as rare as a Soviet/American joint mission into space during the height of the cold war era. It happened, but as very much the exception not the rule.

PART FIVE

Alien Reality

We shall now consider what evidence there may be beyond anecdotal stories to suggest that any of these alien contact claims have really happened.

The big question we all must ask is whether any of them would have taken place as described had you or I been present at the time. Would we have seen what the witness says they saw, or not? A completely sincere person can tell us what they genuinely believe they experienced, just as any of us might report a realistic or vivid dream. But dream reality is quite different from actual reality. To prove the latter, or establish that we really are being visited by strange creatures, requires much more solid evidence than an honest person's self-conviction.

There is a surprising range of what may be considered proof to a greater or lesser degree; although whether this will be convincing or probative in the end may depend upon how liberal-minded you are willing to be.

Clearly the ultimate proof does not exist, for if it did there would be no need for a book like this. The argument would be settled and the truth established. Nevertheless, what we do have is of surprising interest and, if nothing else, challenges those who may by now quite understandably have doubts as to whether there is any physical reality to these alien contacts.

Back-Up Witnesses

In 1989 British researcher John Spencer told a UFO conference in London that he may have evidence of what was then a worrying omission. Whilst by far the majority of abductions are single witness events, there are cases (like the Hills) of a couple abducted together, a few (like Telford, Shropshire) where several friends meet aliens, and even very rare cases where a family of five or six are all involved.

In all of these multi-witness cases there seems to be a relationship, if only close friendship, between the various participants. Nobody was aware of any alien contact that had been witnessed whilst it was taking place by someone who did not know the abductee and was not themselves a part of the encounter.

This is, of course, a critical test of physical reality. For if a bank robbery were to take place on the High Street somebody walking down the road or passing in a car would on occasion see it happen. If all bank robberies were subjective stories told only by their victims we might get suspicious as to whether they were ever really happening.

John Spencer presented a case that he later expanded upon in his fascinating book about abduction investigation (*Perspectives*, MacDonald, 1989).

Anders was the son of an electrician in a country village near Vallentuna, Sweden. Late on the night of 23 March 1974 whilst walking along dark rural roads after a party he saw a column of light rise from a hillock, found a light rushing towards him and threw himself to the ground. He recovered awareness some time later outside his home at Lindholmen. His wife found him upset with cuts and a slight burn.

Subsequently the case was followed up in a largely non-UFO manner, because (particularly in 1974 in such a rural area) there was no social climate for UFO study. But hypnosis was carried out only days after the sighting by Dr Ture Arvidsson at a local hospital. Anders described being sucked up before he struck the ground and arriving in a strange room with 6 feet tall entities. He had an instrument placed against his skin and a mental block preventing further recall, except a promised return visit. He was then 'dropped off at home' by the entities!

In so far as the witness is concerned, this was not an alien contact. He follows the accepted local view that such events describe folklore creatures tied in with earth mysteries and so met beings co-existing on our planet.

John Spencer went to Vallentuna to study the case which he sees as a model to argue that research be witness-led not dictated by the views or beliefs of UFOlogists. His suggestion that it may be an observed abduction comes from the fact that in the twenty-four hours surrounding the encounter there were many local sightings of lights and beams. One woman on a nearby road independently described seeing the same light beside the same hillock at the time when Anders had his encounter.

Of course, this is fascinating. It certainly offers strong support for the view that Anders had an encounter with something that was really present. But *all* it supports is the reality of the light. The alien contact or abduction emerged later from hypnotic regression, as it so often does, and was not verifiable by this uninvolved witness.

Sadly this *cannot* be termed an observed abduction because we still do not know what the woman would have seen had she watched Anders after the lightbeam struck. Would there have been a man on the ground or wandering about dazed or unconscious? Or would she have seen him sucked up into an object as his subsequent hypnotic memory suggested?

Certainly there is other evidence suggesting the reality of the trigger for the alien contact. In the Alan Godfrey case from November 1980, several police officers on moors near Halifax independently reported a blue light heading towards Todmorden at about the same time as the abduction occurred. But here again the support is only limited.

One interpretation of the abduction would be that the policeman's car was stopped by a UFO hovering over a well-used public road, he was then hit by a lightbeam, taken out, examined inside the UFO and deposited back into his car fifteen minutes later. Why, we ask, in case after case such as this, did nobody passing by see the car in the middle of the road with its doors open, even if they did not see the abduction taking place?

It is true that such cases often happen in remote areas and at late hours (the Todmorden abduction was just after 5 a.m.). It is also true that in several longer duration abductions witnesses say under hypnosis that the car was pulled up off the road along with its occupants!

However, surely someone, somewhere, would have been in the right place to observe something, if only by complete accident.

There are five cases on record where an abductee *was* observed during the experience and these are extremely significant. Here are three of them.

A teenage girl from Deeside, North Wales, who had several meetings with Nordics in the mid 1970s, had a fascinating encounter where she vividly saw herself taken from her bedroom in a UFO to see strange plants and animals on the home world of the entities. But we know that this did not happen in our reality, because her mother chanced to go into the bedroom during the encounter and saw her daughter prone on the bed in what resembled a deep sleep or catatonic state. She was sufficiently concerned by this to check later and, finding her now sleeping normally, took no action until the 'abduction' was reported.

A similar case involved housewife Maureen Puddy in Victoria, Australia in 1973. She had had several puzzling UFO contacts and one night was so convinced that something else was going to occur that she went with investigators onto the Mooraduc Road to the site of a prior encounter. Here they saw her get out of the car, apparently seeing a UFO and entity that they could not. In a trance-like state the woman described what took place, culminating in an onboard experience there and then. Still the shocked investigators could only look on in bewilderment. Mrs Puddy was later baffled as to why they saw nothing.

But perhaps the closest duplicate of the Anders story comes from South America. At Fragata Pelotas in Brazil late on 3 March 1978 an eighteen year old man went to check if his father's house was secure for the night when he was struck by a blue beam. He recovered at 4 a.m. and was regressed by a psychologist two weeks later. Here he described a medical encounter inside the UFO with a Nordic female entity. Two men living in this remote area saw a light at this spot that same night. But crucially a third person, walking past, saw the witness unconscious on the ground and left him there, assuming him to be drunk or asleep. This seems to have been during the time of the subsequently recalled abduction.

In these cases we know for certain that the witnesses had not gone anywhere, even though they believed they had an alien contact. Thus we can be sure that at least some abductions *must* only occur on a mental level.

Teleportations

We now know that in some abductions nobody actually goes

anywhere. There is also an alarming lack of back-up witnesses to an alien contact. However, almost in contradiction, there are some cases which seem to come straight out of the pages of a 'Star Trek' novel and imply that the witness not only definitely went somewhere, but in a manner that seems impossible to achieve in an earthly sense.

Here is an example.

In May 1968 Dr Gerardo Vidal and his wife set off from the town of Chascomus, eighty miles south of Buenos Aires, Argentina, to drive 100 miles or so further south to visit relatives in Maipu. Another couple in a car drove with them immediately ahead, but along the way lost track of their friends behind. When this second couple got to Maipu they waited for the Vidals – but they never arrived. Amidst growing concern they retraced the route but the Vidals and their car were nowhere to be seen.

Two days later a phone call was made from an Argentine consulate stating that Dr Vidal and his wife wished to be picked up at the airport. Mrs Vidal was so distressed she had to be hospitalized.

According to Dr Vidal, whilst driving on the road from Chascomus the car was suddenly immersed within a dense fog that appeared out of nowhere and their very next memory is of finding themselves still in the car but on an unknown side road and now in broad daylight. Both witnesses had a pain in their heads and felt extremely tired. As their watches had stopped and they were lost, they asked passers-by where they were but certainly could not have been prepared to be told that they were nowhere near Chascomus. Indeed they were not even in Argentina. In fact this was Mexico, over 4000 miles as the UFO flies and a full continent away!

The consul launched an immediate enquiry. The car was taken away for study. But no answers were found. However, investigators discovered that on the night of this disappearance a man was taken into hospital at Maipu suffering nausea and shock. He said his car had been attacked by a sudden mist that fell from the sky, surrounded his vehicle and then vanished.

Of course, we might sceptically think of all kinds of explanations. But a hoax would be a complicated option. It is impossible that the Vidals could have driven their car to Mexico in forty-eight hours, even travelling all day and night at breakneck speed. It may have been feasible, but surely pointlessly expensive, if they had used air travel. However, if we are to take them at their word this case seems to defy resolution.

What is perhaps more important is that this teleportation does not stand alone. In fact, there is an extraordinarily consistent set of cases remarkably like it.

On 19 November 1963 a bank manager driving a director and client early in the morning along a road outside Tokyo came beside another car at Kanamachi. They saw two occupants and then were amazed to find that it was suddenly surrounded by a white smoke or vapour. After a few moments the fog lifted but the car had totally vanished. Despite attempts to trace the missing vehicle, whatever the occupants may have experienced was never revealed. But the three witnesses are adamant about their story, which does, of course, sound exactly like an outside view of the Vidals' adventure in Argentina.

In October 1974 a family of five travelling home late at night at Aveley in Essex were suddenly plunged into a green mist. The next thing they knew was that there was a bump and they found themselves at a spot half a mile or so down the road and over an hour and a half later. Hypnotic regression in 1977 brought forth the story that the car had been 'beamed' into a UFO and a standard abduction had occurred but without this hypnosis (and its resulting controversial memory or fantasy) the case is just like the Chascomus teleportation. The only difference is that the distances and times involved were rather less.

Three months later, on 5 January 1975, almost identical aliens were met by a railway worker in Bahia Blanca, Argentina. He had been walking home to his wife and child just before 4 a.m. when he was surrounded by a buzzing light and then just found himself in a strange room with these beings. They took hair samples with a suction device and then the man woke up by a roadside at 8 a.m. His watch had stopped at 3.50. A passer by, thinking he had been struck by a car, took him to the local hospital where the police were called in and the real mystery began.

Investigation by police, doctors and psychiatrists found nothing other than apparent truth to this account. The man refused money from the media for his story and just wanted to be reunited with his wife. Twelve hours later he was, but she was forced to travel by train over 300 miles to be there, because he had woken up not where he had departed but outside

Buenos Aires. We do not know how he could have got between these two places in the time available, but he had some proof – a local Bahia Blanca paper that could only be purchased after midnight in that town.

On 8 October 1981 on the remote Isle of Mull in Scotland, the widow of a colonel and a deeply committed Christian was driving with two American tourist friends over the remote Salen Forest when a mist surrounded the car, solidified and encircled it. With it came a heavy pressure and a vibration that shook the metal body. The witnesses were, of course, terrified but it seemed to instantly vanish and the placid summer's day returned to normal. Or almost normal...

The problem was that the sun had moved some way across the sky and so several hours had passed in a trice. They were still on the moors somewhere, disorientated, and both the digital watches worn by the American couple had stopped at the moment when the mist first appeared. A jeweller had to reset them. The car's electrical clock had also stopped.

And still these experiences continue. On the sunny morning of 8 August 1992 a family of four drove from Bedfordshire to Milton Keynes to do some shopping. At Hockliffe they suddenly ran into a bank of mist that appeared from nowhere. The driver and his wife then recall nothing more until they were no longer in the mist and eight miles further down the road near Woburn Sands. Upon arrival in the town they had severe pains, red marks on their skin of unknown origin and a sense of unreality. (Indeed, this was so serious that the woman thought they may have had an accident and died and actually asked a relative later if she was still alive!)

They also experienced great problems getting back to normal reality, a factor we saw in the Maine abduction and in other cases such as the one from Delamere Forest, Cheshire. Both of these had also involved strange mists and clouds.

In the 1992 Hockliffe case the two adults lost bodily coordination for a time and, for example, could not grip the door handle properly when trying to get out of the car. In the Livingston, Scotland contact as you may recall, similar coordination problems were reported and had led the witness to drive his vehicle into a ditch.

This latest case is under investigation by Ken Phillips and Judith Jafaar of BUFORA as I write. There are certainly hints of hidden memories (eg., an Oz factor was present, cars on what should have been a busy road – at mid-morning on a summer Saturday – reputedly just disappeared). It is a very familiar story.

As for the two children (daughters aged five and seven) – they simply recall an unusual quietness descending onto the car, stopping them in mid track for no apparent reason whilst they were merrily singing Beatles songs.

It is not known if one of these songs was 'Help', but in the face of cases like this such an exclamation may seem rather appropriate.

Marks of the Aliens

Late on 18 May 1975 a family at Rainhill, Merseyside, England, spotted three brilliant lights in a triangle drifting over their house. They went out in pursuit and saw what appeared to be a glowing object within a copse. However, after the man who had bravely ventured towards the wood in the dark went back for the others, they all walked into the edge of the trees and found nothing was now there.

At first light an investigation began. The area was muddy around a small pond. The tracks of the witnesses leading to the edge of the area were visible but around the pond nobody had walked (except what seemed to be the prints of a dog). However, there were some very unusual marks.

These appeared to be footprints, but extremely large ones, some 14 inches across and with a stride length of 4 feet between them. Each print was oddly square and very heavily indented. These were photographed for posterity and a stone and a piece of metal embedded into one was taken for analysis by the local Merseyside UFO group.

As is common in such cases little was learnt. The metal was aluminium and the stone had been scuffed by a very heavy pressure. That was about all that could be said. These things could have been important or they may have had nothing to do with the UFO experience. But even if the aliens had left their mark it was impossible to prove anything extraterrestrial about the evidence. Unfortunately, boots made on Alpha Centauri would probably obey just the same laws of physics as those from Bootle. How does one tell the difference?

A similar dilemma occurred in an alien contact at Burneside, Cumbria, in November 1980. The local UFO team could only record the story of a witness who said that two aliens he met whilst walking in the rain had melted his hand held lantern with a 'beam'. The lamp was indeed warped and twisted by heat, as investigators could establish. But analysis could only show that the damage was the result of a heat source akin to a blow-lamp – not whether it really had met its fate at the hands of such an earthly device or whether alien weapons produce the same effect.

Much more common than direct evidence of this type are physical effects reputedly left on the bodies of witnesses. You have already seen frequent references to illnesses post-dating the encounter (which may be a result of the shock) and several to marks such as burns on the skin.

In fact, one of the major criteria that American researchers use to determine whether a case might be an abduction is to discover whether the witness has unexplained puncture wounds or other markings on their bodies in the wake of a puzzling episode. In a high percentage of abductions where medical tests are supposedly carried out by the entities such markings are alleged and can, of course, be photographed and studied. They are thus regarded as prime evidence.

Today such patterns are being reported in cases from all over the world at a prodigious rate. Scant attention seems to have been paid to the possibility that most people have scrape marks, scars or other small painless wounds on arms, legs and skin and for which they do not remember the cause. I know I have such things and as a small experiment decided to ask the first ten people I met at a social gathering (which required some amusing explanations!). Of these we soon found six with marks that these people did not know they had and this was by no means an exhaustive search.

The very act of self scrutiny or examination by investigators who are expecting to find evidence on a witness suspected of being an abductee must lead to a spurious increase in such apparent evidence.

This is not to imply that this evidence is always invalid. Merely a cautionary warning that we should not overemphasize what for too many has become a key element of those claims alleging that abductees really are physically examined by aliens.

That said, there are some baffling cases. A renowned biological scientist from southern France was struck by a beam of light from a UFO whilst on the balcony of his rural home in November 1968. His baby son was nearby. The doctor later experienced strange memories suggesting an alien contact and also developed a red triangle on his abdomen which could be photographed. At the same time, although then miles away from the doctor and staying with relatives, the young child developed the same triangle. I asked French scientist Dr Jacques Vallee about this case in April 1992. It seems that twenty years on the triangle was still visible on both witnesses; although at times more prominent than at others.

Aliens in Camera

There are literally thousands of photographs that supposedly show UFOs. A few are hoaxes, but many are film faults or other images that happen to look UFO-like. Most are other things, e.g., balloons or stars, and these an investigator terms IFOs (*identified* flying objects). If the human eye can be fooled by something misleading in the sky, then so, of course, can a camera. Indeed, sometimes it can be even more deceived, because a camera freezes a fraction of a second onto emulsion. An object that may not normally seem odd, such as a bird in flight, can appear extremely weird when transfixed by chance at just the right moment.

To my knowledge nobody has ever taken a photograph during an abduction showing the inside of a UFO. This adds fuel to those who believe these events are never real in any physical sense, but it must be admitted that taking photographs is unlikely to be on someone's mind should they find themselves in the middle of these events. In any case, the stories strongly imply that the aliens control the memory and thinking processes of the witness, so the taking of photographs would probably not be an acceptable possibility.

Nevertheless, there are about ten cases on record where someone has allegedly photographed an alien entity. Several of them can be dismissed from all consideration as fraud pure and simple; at least two (from Germany in the 1950s) being April Fool's media hoaxes which have taken on a credibility that they certainly do not deserve. An often published picture is a table top model and in another often touted case, the landed UFO was created by a sewage pipe in the garden and a doll suitably kitted out in silver clothes. The whole thing was then illuminated by a flashlight and the imaginative result presented by a young boy from North Carolina. It certainly had some UFO experts fooled for a while!

Given the potential importance of this material it is worth examining those few remaining pieces of visual evidence that are not quite so easy to dispose of.

24 May 1964   Cumbria, England

Fireman Jim Templeton was taking pictures of his daughter on a quiet marsh. It was a warm, sunny day. He saw nothing unusual through the lens of his Pentacon camera. Nor did his wife and other daughter who were nearby. After processing, an odd 'man' was found on one of the shots. He was semi-transparent, seemingly wearing a spacesuit and appearing behind the head and shoulder of the girl. No real person had been on the marsh and close examination of the photograph shows that the figure is either extremely tall or, if normally proportioned, floating above the ground.

Kodak, who developed the pictures, tried every way to figure it out, as did the police. Suspicion fell on an accidental double exposure, i.e., two negatives superimposed on top of each other during printing. But this was ruled out when analysis showed that the figure is blocked out by the girls head, following normal laws of optics in a way a superimposition could not do. Ultimately, Kodak offered free film for life to anyone who could solve the mystery. Nobody ever claimed this prize.

In 1990 the picture was blown up life-size as part of a gimmick for a local copying firm. This exercise revealed ears behind a transparent visor and breathing tubes around the back. Certainly if this picture is nothing more than a freak result of light and shadow or an emulsion defect, as some sceptics suggest, it is a coincidence as amazing as the proverbial monkey typing out the works of Shakespeare by chance.

Of course, the Templetons saw no UFO and this is a strange suited human-like figure, not obviously an alien. However, when I spoke to the photographer in 1990 (and no UFOlogists had bothered before) I found that there was a fascinating and unreported sequel. After the pictures were developed two men arrived in a dark Jaguar car and took Jim for a meeting on the marsh. They showed cards and claimed to be government investigators. Then they asked some very unusual questions about the behaviour of local animals at the time, becoming annoyed when he refused to accept their suggestion that the picture was just an ordinary man on the fields. They drove off, leaving him to walk five miles home.

Although Jim Templeton appeared not to know this fact, his story is a classic tale of the so-called 'Men in Black' who have visited many of the witnesses to alien contact and behaved in exactly this manner.

18 February 1967   Massachusetts, USA

Mrs Stella Lansing from Palmer is what UFOlogists call a 'repeater witness', having seen countless UFOs over many years. This led her to take quite a few photographs with relatively poor camera and film, until in 1966 she borrowed an 8 mm movie camera from her boss (a jeweller). About four months later the opportunity arose to use it on a snow-bound night.

At first Mrs Lansing saw only strange orange and yellow balls near powerlines, one bouncing on the ground. She drove home and brought the camera to the site, where she proceeded to film along with another local resident who came by in her car to watch the lights. They both observed for a couple of minutes until the one object that was left drifted away.

Upon projection, the developed reel was a major surprise. It showed a light, as expected, but also several 'people' in the foreground who seemed to be inside or in front of a more dimly visible room. About five seconds of film clearly show them and have since been analysed.

However, again there is a disappointment. These are not like aliens discussed in this book. Indeed they resemble three human males wearing normal clothes (one even has a moustache) and the effect is rather like a scene from TV accidentally superimposed onto the image of the UFO.

From the investigation of the site and case by psychiatrist, Dr Berthold Schwarz, there seems little doubt of its veracity, but what does the film show? He speculated about 'thoughtography' (ie., images 'projected' onto film as some psychics have claimed they can do). Given later paranormal experiences and strange non-UFO photographs obtained during experiments with Mrs Lansing, this seems less silly than it sounds.

Dr Schwarz could not accept the possibility of a deliberate

hoax by the witness. On the other hand, scientists who were offered the film for deeper study just would not look at it. This is a reaction I have seen in other cases. Yet surely hard evidence such as this should be exactly what scientists desire for investigation, whatever the ultimate outcome?

Berthold Schwarz discusses this case and his years of dedicated research in his quarter of a million word book *Psychiatric and Psychic Aspects of the UFO Syndrome* (Rainbow, 1983) which is all too poorly known even by UFOlogists in his native USA.

17 October 1973   Alabama, USA

At last we come upon a case where something that resembles the witness accounts of alien contact was actually filmed. However, once again it is not as straightforward as all that.

During a major UFO wave that included the infamous Pascagoula abduction, police officer Jeff Greenhaw at Falkville received a phone call from a woman that a flashing UFO had been seen to land nearby. He drove to the scene, taking a polaroid camera with him.

When he got there neither woman nor UFO was visible but a tall figure in a silver suit with an antenna on its head was looming ahead of him in the darkness. Coolly Jeff jumped out and took four pictures as the figure moved stiffly about. These clearly show exactly what he reported – a 6 foot tall entity encased in a reflective suit with no facial features. Then, as the witness switched on the revolving light on top of his patrol car, the figure ran off down a side road into the night.

The policeman scrambled back into the car and gave pursuit. In the dark this was very difficult as the road was little more than a rutted track. He could only reach 20 mph but reports that the figure outpaced him! In his increasingly frustrated attempts to catch up the officer strayed off the road and had to abandon the chase.

Given the wave of UFO interest the story achieved local publicity. It was then that the problems really began. Greenhaw suffered a spate of misfortunes, ranging from threatening phone calls to his mobile home strangely burning down. Eventually he quit and moved away, causing some to speculate that he may have been 'set up' by elements wishing to discredit him. As a good policeman there must have been less salubrious residents who would have preferred that he not discharge his duties. It is also quite possibly significant that only the day before in Ohio three youths dressed up in silver foil and an antenna and were caught walking along a road scaring traffic. Did this story give someone else the idea?

We may never know, because the case, evidently genuine as it is, involves nothing other than a figure in a silver suit. There is no way of deducing from these photographs whether that figure is a human being attempting to hoax the policeman or a visitor from the beyond that he was able to film.

November 1987–March 1988   Florida, USA

This complex case has been the hot issue of the UFO community for six years and remains contentious. The fact that it has attracted massive publicity, a book written by the two key witnesses, for which some UFO experts were reportedly paid, and has undoubtedly proved lucrative, may or may not detract from its credibility according to your viewpoint. Unfortunately, in this day and age there is nothing to stop a genuine 'big story' making people money, but equally, given the public's desire to believe and the willingness of the media to promote such a belief, we have to anticipate that occasionally a few clever hoaxes must occur.

Claim and counter claim, proof and disproof, have all been marshalled by rival UFO teams and who is right remains confused. All we can note is that Ed and Frances Walters (as of early 1993) stand by their 1990 book *The Gulf Breeze Sightings* and insist that the dozens of colour photographs and the video film that they took are genuine. Some big names in American UFO research have supported them, mostly, they say, because the couple obtained photographs using a specially built stereo camera provided by photographic expert Dr Bruce Maccabee. That was in the midst of an incredible five month sequence of filming glittering UFOs night after night. In June 1992 Dr Maccabee showed me video film that he personally took at Gulf Breeze the month before.

Whilst the Walters (and now others in the town) saw and filmed UFOs regularly, visits by 4 feet tall aliens, including a claimed time loss abduction affecting Ed Walters on the shore, sadly could not be so preserved. However, something almost as interesting was.

On 24 January 1988 Ed Walters was video filmed by journalist Duane Cook as they drove in search of more UFOs. Although Cook filmed none, Walters alleged to hear a 'buzz' in his head which he considered a sign they were around. On the resultant film he is seen struggling in apparent pain pleading with 'them' to stop this torture. Alien contact 'live' as it happens has never been claimed on film before. Ed then got out, said he saw the UFO, took one polaroid shot, but this was sadly not filmed. It was visible for moments only and Cook had just decided it was too dark to shoot. But he confirms what happened and personally developed the film seconds later, as yet another shot of the UFO came out of Ed's polaroid.

1 December 1987   Ilkley Moor, England

This is undoubtedly the most amazing alien photograph so far, but sadly, like all the rest, it has flaws. However, it also has unique advantages.

It began when I received a letter the first week in December 1987. It came from a former police officer who had found my address from a book in the library and wanted to report his extraordinary story. He claimed to have visual evidence of an alien taken less than forty-eight hours earlier. He gave his real name (which offered a startling coincidence, but I cannot elaborate as this may reveal his identity). But he had to be contacted via a box number hundreds of miles away. I tried to track him down but discovered that he had moved the day before I got the letter. Although I did write, cautiously yet openmindedly, to the given box number right away, the witness says he could not check for a reply for some time and got fed up with waiting. So he found another more liberal UFOlogist from the library, sent his full address and also gave him the photograph.

By coincidence, after an initial interview that UFOlogist was happy with the story and not very interested in deep research. He invited my colleague Peter Hough to take it on. As I had already shown Peter the letter of some four weeks before he realized this was the same case and immediately set to work with the witness. A major investigation followed, for which much of the credit must go to Peter. Whilst at first we were both intensely sceptical that this case could possibly be real, most of what followed only enhanced the strength of the story.

Very briefly, Philip Spencer (pseudonym) was walking over Ilkley Moor just before dawn on 1 December 1987. His aim was to photograph the early light over the mill villages from the moor tops. Upon our request, Philip immediately provided us with all negatives from the relevant film which show that he had indeed photographed bridges and stone buildings on earlier days. So this story did at least have an element of credibility.

He took a compass to guide him in the dark and used high ASA rated low light film. This was necessary given the dim winter's light but as a result makes the unexpected shot rather fuzzy and grainy.

At the White Wells area, which has local folklore associations with strange creatures, he saw a weird entity on the slopes ahead. He took one quick picture as it gestured at him (to get back) and then it ran off.

Recovering composure Philip says he scrambled after it and was just in time to see a domed object with a white box on top rise from behind an outcrop and shoot skywards. He did not photograph this. Leaving his pursuit he walked the thirty minutes down to civilization and noted two things. His compass now pointed south instead of north and the town clock showed more than an hour later than it ought to have done. He began to snap pictures quickly to use up film, then realized the futility and took a bus to the nearest main town where he could get the prints developed instantly. Sure enough he had one shot of the strange, blue/green covered and dome-headed entity that he had seen a few hours before. He then found my address and wrote that letter.

The investigation of this case was very sophisticated as we tried all we could to establish the facts on what is a story few – even in the UFO world – can easily accept. It is in a sense too good to be true, especially occurring as it did parallel to (but when nobody in Britain knew about) the Gulf Breeze photographs.

We had the alien picture examined by a wildlife photography expert. It was not an animal but we could not establish if it was animate or static. A site reconstruction showed that whatever it was had been about 4½ feet tall. Peter Hough also had the photograph studied by the Kodak laboratories in Hemel Hempstead, who concluded it was a real image of something on the rocks, not trick photography. Another independent study at a photo lab occurred before the picture went to the USA for computer enhancement. I spoke with Dr Bruce Maccabee, an optical physicist with the US navy about his assessment. Sadly the image was too grainy to allow proper study, which, as Dr Maccabee told me, was 'very disappointing, because I had great hopes that this case would prove definitive. Sadly circumstances prevent it from being so.' However, the enhanced images have been seized upon by a few less cautious researchers as showing detail such as ears that, frankly, owe more to creative imagination than they do to what the fuzzy enhanced resolution allows.

There is a curiosity on the film. A white square appears on the hill at exactly the point where Philip Spencer says the UFO was then obscured by the rockface. Nothing is actually at that spot. He did not point this out and when Peter and I first asked him if he thought it might be the top of the UFO behind the hillock he was typically non-committal.

Peter also arranged for a university to test the compass. It had been within a strong magnetic field to alter its polarity. But using a magnetic resonance scanner at a hospital, the effect could be duplicated so a hoax remained feasible. However, if it was a hoax it required rather more effort than the usual trick shot of a button held in the sky.

Much else was done, such as using another university to do radiation and magnetic tests on the rocks (all negative). Philip Spencer was studied by a clinical psychologist, who was convinced he was telling the truth. Finally, when all other work was concluded, he was hypnotically regressed and came out with a memory of being abducted, medically examined and shown imagery in a tale much like so many others. Under hypnosis Philip reported that the photograph was really taken after the abduction had ended, when he was put back on the moors and the entity was scurrying away.

This might explain the only major problem which emerged during study (and which Philip Spencer never tried to obscure, stating only that he could not account for it). Given the position of the sun and weather on 1 December 1987 the photograph could not have been taken at the time when the witness first said it had. However, if the hypnotic memory is correct and it was in fact taken ninety minutes later than he believed then the image is consistent with the lighting conditions at that point.

It is worth stressing that by 1993 Peter Hough had formed a strong long term rapport with the witness, meeting him often and considering him trustworthy. I have met him too and in more normal circumstances probably would not doubt his testimony. He has made no money from what many might regard as the most significant photo of the century, nor has he sought any publicity. Indeed he signed over copyright to Peter Hough in early 1988 and later gave him the camera that was used because, he said, he wanted the picture discussed openly but did not wish anyone to think he was trying to capitalise on it. He also feared personal attention might damage his desire to re-join the police force.

Even with by far the most impressive photographic evidence for an alien we are left with uneasy imperfection. The witness seems sincere, although his interest level seems somewhat more muted than I would expect. And seeing a fuzzy image of a 'little green man' does sound alarm bells of disquiet. Sadly nobody can say if we have a picture of a 4½ foot tall youth in a suit, a dummy someone placed on the moor or a real alien.

Gifts from the Stars

In one of the very first abductions Betty Hill had tried to snatch a book from inside the UFO to prove that she had really been within this strange craft. She was denied, but surely if, as alleged, thousands of people have met aliens and many of these have spent an hour or more on board a device from an advanced civilization then someone, somewhere, would by now have grabbed hold of one item of tangible proof.

There are very good landing cases where burns, holes, even chemical changes in the cell structure of plants have been recorded. But these show only that an energy force was present, not any alien intelligence. We need hard evidence, as with photographs, that could establish the truth of actual alien contact beyond any reasonable doubt. Does it exist?

Bits that Fell Off

On 24 April 1950 forty-two year old factory worker Bruno Facchini went out for a breath of air after the late night storm that struck Varese in northern Italy. He spotted some flashes lighting up the sky and assumed that lightning might have affected the power lines, so went to investigate. What he saw was not lightning but a dome-shaped object with a ladder. At the top of this, surrounded by greenish light, was a fair-skinned being of normal or slightly taller than human size, dressed in a diving suit and apparently welding the metal surface of the craft.

Facchini thought he was watching an aircraft from one of the nearby military bases and so decided to offer assistance to what were in fact several similar individuals. He got no reply but heard a buzzing noise 'like a gigantic beehive' and saw the ladder being raised into the circular object. Now realizing he was watching no aircraft he ran. However, he had barely moved before one of the entities pointed a tube at him and a beam of light emerged. Bruno reports that he fell to the ground like he had been hit with a jet of compressed air, crashing onto a marker stone at the edge of the field.

As he lay there bruised and sore the entities got on with their task and simply ignored him. After a moment they went into the device and there was a sudden increase in the buzzing noise. The object then shot skywards and vanished.

Next day the witness reported the matter to the police and went back to the site. Here he found burnt patches and indentations on the ground and some peculiar pieces of metal. Thinking these must be bits left over from the alien welding operation he picked them up. They were shiny with a granular surface. The witness took them to be analysed and claims he was told that they were 'anti-friction' metal.

In September 1953 UFO investigators had an independent test carried out on the remaining metal at a scientific institute specialising in metallurgy. Their report describes them as yellow/white, weighing 1.64 grams and comprising 74 per cent copper, 19 per cent tin and other metals in smaller quantities. It was, they concluded, 'leaded bronze' which had an 'entirely normal' micrographic structure. In other words, if these were bits of alien waste metal they were sadly very terrestrial in nature and nothing exotic could be established about them.

Unhappily, this was a pattern to be repeated in a handful of future cases where bits of metal were found at a UFO site. They were always very mundane. Indeed, in no other case were they as clearly linked with the UFO as they were here or ever again directly associated with alien entities.

The only case where there is any substantial evidence for an alien metal is itself flawed. A letter with an illegible signature was sent to a newspaper reporting that three fishermen had seen a UFO crash towards the sea at Ubatuba, Brazil, on 10 September 1957. At the last moment it halted its decline, turned sharply upwards and exploded, showering metal into the ocean. A few bits fell on the beach and were sent to the paper, but despite extensive efforts no eyewitness was ever found.

UFOlogist Dr Olavo Fontes took the fragments to an internationally known chemist at a top government lab. Here the samples were split and several independent tests followed. These employed extensive techniques including spectographic and atomic structure analyses. The surprising conclusions from these were that the metal was exceptionally pure magnesium with a faint surface coating of magnesium hydroxide.

This was not only consistent with the story of the object descending at speed through the atmosphere but in 1957 no techniques existed in Brazil to make magnesium that was as pure as the analysed sample. Unfortunately the piece for which the results were obtained was consumed by the various test processes, but two other pieces remained.

In the USA it was later found that these remaining pieces, whilst still very pure, were not as pure as the results claimed for the original sample in Brazil. In 1969 a US government study carried out by chemist Dr Roy Craig for the University of Colorado found minute quantities of strontium in one fragment, which, although highly unusual, was not inconsistent with American experimental techniques in force during 1957.

In the 1970s the dwindling amounts of this unique UFO evidence were subjected to more tests thanks to our ever improving technology. It was found that the crystal structure was of a type well suited to spaceflight but only then being experimented with in laboratories. In 1957 not only did the technology not exist to align the crystals in this way but the concept had yet to be invented. Although some dispute that.

The most recent experiments during the 1980s, described by Australian industrial chemist and UFO trace expert Bill Chalker, have probed the exact metal isotopes to be found within the magnesium. Whilst these are unusual they turn out to be ones that do exist on earth. It is impossible to argue that they could not have been produced here.

Once again the evidence fails to establish any true extraterrestrial origin for what seems like vital evidence.

However, in the Ubatuba case there is at least a fighting chance that this debris may have come from an unknown source beyond the earth. Sadly it seems unlikely that this will ever be proven and the absence of any subsequent materials of even closely similar nature or calibre of evidence must be of concern to those who support the physical reality of alien contact.

Alien Artifacts

On the morning of 18 April 1961, a sixty year old farmer called Joe Simonton claimed that a silvery disc landed in his farmyard at Eagle River, Wisconsin. Three fairly ordinary-looking but small men in blue one-piece suits were inside and one handed Joe a silver jug through a hatch. From gestures he worked out that they wanted him to go and fill it with something and he assumed they needed water. Ever the hospitable sort he went and topped up the jug and handed it back. Inside the UFO he saw one of them cooking 'pancakes with holes' over a flameless hotplate. He motioned that he would like one and was given four. The object then shot away leaving the farmer with the only known examples of gourmet cookery from another world.

Absurd as this story does sound, it has the kind of naive incredibility that many alien contacts seem to possess. Indeed the theme of seeking water was an oddly common one, just as it was an often used excuse in fairy folklore when the elementals would initiate an interaction with humanity.

Simonton, who soon got fed up with the laughter he appears not to have expected from his story, seemed mostly upset that 'they' never spoke to him, despite his friendliness at their intrusion.

Of the four pancakes, he ate one and said it tasted like cardboard. An investigator who later nibbled at another said it was more like corn. Simonton retained one and after the amused response and distinct lack of concern by UFOlogists of the day refused to hand it over. But he did give one to a UFO group. As they were disinterested in it they passed it onto another group, APRO. The final pancake was given to Dr J Allen Hynek, then the science consultant to the US air force. He had it analysed at his own North Western University in Chicago.

The results were not dramatic. The object was a pretty dire mixture of flour, sugar and grease, none of which were of

obviously extraterrestrial origin. Based on these findings
APRO secretary Coral Lorenzen set about some of the most
unusual of all UFO experiments, to recreate the pancakes in
her kitchen. She eventually found a combination that did look
just like them.

If this case is hardly going to set the scientific world alight,
none of the examples of alien artifacts that have followed have
been much of an improvement.

An extraordinary case was investigated in great depth by Philip
Taylor, an excellent BUFORA UFOlogist and mathematician
(then at the Greenwich Observatory).

Edwin, the witness, was a retired military figure and scientist
of some standing, specialising in audiology (hearing). He lived
at the time of the experiences in an evocative rural spot at
Sedlescombe, near Hastings, Sussex.

During 1966 and earlier in 1967 Edwin had found several
flattened circles in a grass field beyond his home. But then,
between 17 August and 23 September 1967, the witness says he
had no fewer than nine visits by aliens. On the first occasion he
met them whilst out walking with his dogs and invited them in.
On later occasions they simply turned up in the house; always
in the early hours after midnight. They communicated with
each other by whistles and twittering noises but at no point
spoke to Edwin, except by gestures.

The object from which they emerged was conical and resting
on three legs. At no time did he see it land and in later visits the
beings prevented him from going out to look at it. They literally
carried him back into his house as indication that they did not
wish him to watch them depart.

The entities themselves were exceptionally thin and only just
over five feet tall. Their skin was described as 'grey like
parchment' and they seemed to have no body hair at all. He
had ample time to study them closely as they stayed for an hour
or so at a time (once watching TV with him!). Their lips were
almost invisible and their ears just a horny ring inset into the
head. Their hands felt like 'withered leaves' and had only three
fingers and a thumb. They wore tight-fitting wetsuits with
balaclava helmets and always came into the house in pairs.

This description is, of course, remarkably akin to the 'greys'
of recent abduction lore. Although when Edwin first recounted
his story to us (1982) these were becoming a part of the UFO

record they were much less well known, especially amongst the British public.

However, research by Philip Taylor has found a person that Edwin reported his story to in 1967. She was traced in a new location after some effort and confirmed the story. Various other details checked out as well. These clearly established that, whatever the status of this case, Edwin clearly first told of his meetings with these entities at a time when the Greys were almost unheard of even in UFO literature.

During their visits to his home Edwin claims they took samples of many things, being particularly interested in fruit. They even had sips of whisky and showed great distaste! On their penultimate visit they reputedly stayed in the garden taking samples of shrubs and bushes. Another time they motioned that they wanted to take his dog with them. Alien interest in dogs is, in fact, a strangely common fetish. Edwin placated them by offering two china model dogs instead. They took these.

His only attempt at real communication was when he drew a sketch of the solar system and asked them to mark it. They noted a spot outside the orbits of all the planets, which he took to mean they were from another star system.

On the ninth visit Edwin decided to defy their ban on watching their departure. He went out a while after they had left and noted a blue glow coming from beneath the object. It did not take off as he expected but simply disappeared on the spot. This was the last time he saw them.

However, before they left they had given him two gifts. One was a few seeds which they told him to plant. He did so and something resembling a flowering cactus with a single thick and spikeless stump grew from the pot. He sketched it but did not photograph it and it was long dead by the time he reported this to us.

Luckily the situation was different with his other gift. These were tiny bits of crystal that superficially resembled uncut diamonds. Thinking this might be what they were he sent one for analysis by a London diamond merchant. Edwin proved he had done this, providing the report that was sent back. The specific gravity of the crystal was 2.64 and the merchant's comments were that 'the most probable identification is quartz'. Edwin made no bones about this deflating diagnosis, which he openly told us about, expressing bemusement as to why his visitors had offered such meaningless proof of their status. But Philip Taylor arranged for a further analysis just to be sure.

R.K. Harrison of the Institute of Geological Studies in London kindly examined the crystals and stated, 'your specimen is a piece of glassy quartz – silicon dioxide – certainly not extraterrestrial I am sorry to say.'

Philip Taylor was impressed by the witness and his straightforward presentation of a seemingly ridiculous story and its absurd physical proof. He ultimately commented, 'I have not been able to disprove anything that Edwin has claimed, neither have I been able to prove that anything unusual happened. This series of entity encounters must remain as simply a sincerely believed experience.'

The same could be said about most other cases.

Precisely why this type of evidence always seems to self-destruct we do not know. But it is a fact of the records which cannot be ignored.

In January 1988 a family of five travelling by car from Perth, Western Australia, towards Adelaide, reported that they were 'attacked' by an egg-like object which sucked them up off the road before crashing them down again, bursting a tyre in the process and sending them slewing off the road. This was in a remote spot on the Eyre Highway near Mundrabilla.

The case became world famous as it chanced to coincide with Australia's bicentennial celebrations. Whilst no aliens were alleged by the witnesses, a mysterious powder was said to be scattered over the car which smelt badly. Unfortunately, later investigations of this material were only to add typical confusion to the affair.

One group of UFOlogists later vacuumed samples from the vehicle and claimed that analyses suggested an unusual chemical composition. They cited test results that included materials used in protective substances that aided heat resistance in spacecraft. But another group had their own samples tested and these were found to contain nothing more than what was said to be worn lining from the brake system of the car. Police also took samples before anybody else and although they did not publish what they had concluded, Australian UFOlogist Keith Basterfield tells me he has established that they also found nothing unearthly in these traces.

However sincere this UFO report may well have been, once more what started off as promising evidence for an alien substance has faded.

As I write (early 1993) a new case is under investigation where a man and wife had a terrifying encounter in the Quantock Hills of Somerset. The story is very complex and it would be premature to conclude anything about it at this stage, except to note that one witness says he was made ill after a close encounter which he actually photographed whilst it was happening. Later the UFO flew over his garden and immediately afterwards he and his wife found an object which they believe may have been dropped. Despite fears about radiation emission they put this into their fish tank for safe keeping!

This peculiar object is a rocky mass about the size of a small fist, somewhat shiny and crystaline but dark green in colour. Once again it superficially resembles glassy quartz on initial examination. A full assessment of this physical evidence and the other details of this extraordinary case will be pending for some time. Preliminary results suggest it is a form of plastic, ironically like that used to make artificial rocks in a fish tank! It seems that we are yet again heading into a situation where the proof that the aliens offer up to a witness is found to be no proof of anything at all.

Some researchers, despairing that we will ever discover something that is truly 'out of this world', have speculated that these things may be quite deliberate. Perhaps these samples are purposefully mundane in nature so as to tantalise and tease but never to establish that definitive proof.

Of course, sceptics may argue that 'they would say that, wouldn't they?' It comes down to the old question in so far as aliens are concerned as to whether absence of evidence constitutes evidence of absence or something rather stranger than that.

Alien Implants

Although most examples of extraterrestrial substances that have been claimed are connected with ordinary UFO sightings and just occasionally with alien contacts, none relate to abductions. Nobody has, to my knowledge, returned from an alleged trip inside a UFO with anything that they say they picked up whilst onboard. This may, of course, be further grounds to suggest that these events never happen in literal reality but are instead a form of visionary experience.

However, in the past few years the abduction story has developed its own form of physical evidence with the increase in reports that an implant has been put inside the body of a witness during time spent with the aliens. This implant is usually described as a small round ball and acts as some sort of control or monitoring device. It is rarely said to cause any discomfort and witnesses are usually unsure where it is. Entry point is often described as the nose and unexpected violent nose bleeds covering the bedclothes in the morning are now considered by some UFOlogists to be a further symptom of unrecalled abduction.

In fact, the first hints of implants go back to the early 1970s; although it was the following decade before witnesses began to claim in large numbers that things were being placed inside them by aliens. In almost all cases the memory only emerges through hypnosis.

Stories, of course, are just stories, but technology has now become well enough advanced that, hard as it may be to find these so-called implants, they are no longer inaccessible to the wonders of science. We can search for them. By all expectations by now we should have found at least one of them.

In fact we have, but as you will no doubt anticipate, such discoveries have posed more questions than they have provided answers.

A woman from Adelaide, South Australia, approached Keith Basterfield with a story of her life-long meetings with aliens, beginning in about 1971 when she was a ten year old child.

The entities were described as comprising a single taller being and several smaller greys; with all the usual features of large eyes, hairless skin and slit mouths. The larger being was almost 7 feet tall and seemed to have control over the smaller entities who at various points carried out medical examinations.

These abductions took place from her bedroom and she returned to her bed afterwards, which is a common scenario. Most of the details of her experiences have come by way of subsequent regression hypnosis sessions.

The case takes on its unusual status when her hypnotic

testimony referred to an object being implanted into her face during the medical examination by the aliens.

Whilst the background to this case has proved fascinating to the investigator, noting that she was a victim of childhood abuse, and that she has also reported lifelong psychic experiences such as poltergeist activity and levitation, it was the physical evidence which set this case apart. Could the implant be found?

Using dental X-rays an object was seen on one of the exposures in the side of the mouth. Unfortunately, when a more detailed and larger exposure of this same area was later taken the dark blurred anomaly disappeared and its existence has failed to be confirmed ever since.

In other words, once again what seems like a significant discovery crumbles as soon as deeper investigation is carried out. But what was photographed in the first place? Was it merely a shadow on the X-ray plate as some specialists argue? If so, is it not a coincidence that it appeared where the implant was expected to be? But how can it be a real object when detailed searches since have failed to find it?

In almost every case in the USA where an implant has been sought no sign of one has been found. Using magnetic resonance scanners it is now possible to take a photograph of a person's head and seek objects that might be in there. Unfortunately, this is an expensive process and has been rarely possible so far. Doctors are not queuing up to use hospital resources looking for alien artifacts inside someone's head!

The Ultimate Case?

The Holy Grail of believers in alien contact has always been the definitive case; the one that would have so much clout that it would finally convince the world that ET *has* landed.

This has proved hopelessly elusive. In two polls taken of UFOlogists during 1980 (by Ronald Story in the USA) and 1986 (by myself in Britain) almost nobody was willing to stake their reputation on any single case. Indeed there was hardly any consensus on which cases were the best, the list being almost as long as the number of researchers who were surveyed. In addition, many of the classic cases that most experts cited (e.g., the McMinnville, Oregon, photos from 1950, the Lakenheath/Bentwaters, England radar and military jet chase of 1956 or the Trans-en-Provence, France landing of 1981) are all highly impressive but do not clearly demonstrate an alien presence, just unrecognized physical phenomena.

However, from 1987 onwards there has been a dramatic turnaround. Suddenly UFOlogy has been hit by a barrage of major cases, all involving alien contact. It began with the incredible worldwide success of Whitley Strieber's New York state abduction claims which throughout that year became the best known UFO case of all time around the world. Here it was mostly the prior fame and reputation of the witness, not anything unique about the case, which caught the public imagination.

A year later came the dramatic revelation of the still hotly argued Gulf Breeze, Florida photographs. Whatever their status, repetitive visits and multiple photographs of a UFO whilst it is allegedly involved in landings, alien contacts and abductions was quite unheard of and – a key reason why some UFOlogists were instantly sceptical – it flew directly in the face of all that we had learnt about the phenomenon's behaviour. Things just had never happened like that in UFOlogy before.

At the same time a former police officer walking on Ilkley Moor went through an abduction and photographed his captor in a case that again defied tradition, thus raising doubts, but was not readily disproven.

In 1989 even the once staid and utterly unsensational Soviet news agency TASS told the world that an alien contact in a Russian park was real and, once again, had physical evidence in its support.

Some even argue that the appearance of crop circle patterns that have entranced billions of people all over the globe since 1989 is another indication. It is true that many former UFOlogists have defected to become 'cereologists' actively studying these marks, not convinced (incorrectly in my view) that they are an alien communication.

Coupled with the constant stream of revelations about the landing and alien contact outside a NATO air base in Suffolk in late 1980 these events do seem to have reinforced that apparently absurd concept of an 'education programme'. It is almost as if we are gradually being led one more step up the stairway with cases coming thick and fast that add new status to the evidence. These all go completely against previous patterns. One is almost pushed towards the conclusion that someone, somewhere, must be slowly escalating the quality of proof that is associated with the UFO mystery – but in a way that is never quite perfect.

In the past, UFOlogy owed its strength to thousands of cases happening every year which singly were far from conclusive but taken together were an impressive body of testimony. This has all changed. UFO groups the world over have reported general sighting totals falling to levels far below any previously known. Yet at the same moment individual cases of extraordinary nature are acting upon public credibility in a different way. For some, it suggests that the aliens have employed a new tactic and that this switch in battle plans is to appear less often but much more overtly – yet still not quite offering absolute proof, only something a point or two below that level.

Of course, there are those who quite properly caution that not all information is good information. It is possible to think of other sources rather than the UFO phenomenon itself that might want to manufacture a new order of evidence. Scientific sceptics have become belligerent. There are suspicions that at times they might set up cases to be later exposed and thus show the folly of the expert. Government disinformation can not be ruled out in such matters. Or perhaps occasionally hoaxers may realize that more sophistication is required to attract attention.

However, it was no great surprise that in 1991 news began to filter around the hierarchy of UFOlogy that 'the big one' had finally happened and that when the time was right this would be revealed. Then the world would no longer be in any doubt. One renowned expert told me when we met in the USA in June 1992 that when this case became known to the man and woman in the street everything would change overnight.

As I am finally free to discuss this event you can judge for yourself whether this optimism was justified and if the latest step up UFOlogy's 'Everest' is indeed the ultimate ladder or just another snake.

Linda was already an abductee when the so-called 'case of the century' happened to her. She had had experiences since childhood and had contacted abduction specialist Budd Hopkins in April 1989 after reading one of his books. Of course, in here she could read the full abduction scenario. Hopkins had, in his usual kind and sincere way, taken Linda under his wing and worked tirelessly to bring out memories of several visits into a UFO during her life through the use of regression hypnosis.

However, when she called seven months later from her high rise appartment in central Manhattan it was to report that the experiences, which both thought had ended years before, were back with a vengeance.

Her conscious recall contained just snatches. She had worked late around the flat and went to bed very tired at 3 a.m. Then she became numb – a warning sign she knew from prior experiences. One of the typical 'greys' (small, large-headed with round black eyes) appeared by her bed and she was able to attack it by throwing a pillow. Then she became totally paralysed and next recalled being on the usual table undergoing some medical procedure inside the UFO, before being back in bed.

Under hypnosis she came out with one of the most chilling abduction claims – of literally being floated through her closed apartment window by several of the entities. Here she saw herself hanging twelve storeys above the New York streets suspended in a beam of light along with her attendants. Then she was pulled into the hovering disc-like craft where she underwent the standard medical examination. On return she was 'dropped' onto the bed from mid-air and suffered trauma as her husband and young children could not be woken. She thought the aliens had killed them, but proved that they were breathing by holding a mirror up to them.

Linda became a regular in Budd Hopkins' self-help therapy sessions in New York where abductees get together to comfort one another and share each other's tales (a similar idea is operated in London by researcher Ken Phillips). However, the case would have become swamped by the growing tide of similar abductions but for a letter received by Hopkins in February 1991 – some fifteen months after the abduction.

It came from two men who gave their first names only and professed to be police officers. They described how at 3 a.m. on that night in late November 1989 they had been parked on duty at a named spot in Manhattan when they saw an oval object hovering above apartments nearby. They then described in exact detail the story of how Linda was seen to be floated out of her window and into the UFO. This took off and dived into the river, from which, despite staying forty-five minutes, they never saw it emerge.

The men, Richard and Dan, claimed to be ashamed that they could do nothing to save the woman and were living with terrible guilt, which soon afterwards drove one of them into psychiatric care. They explained that they knew where the woman lived, had watched the apartment and were trying to get the courage to go and see if the woman really existed, was alive, dead or if they had simply imagined what they saw.

During the next two years Budd Hopkins made attempts to interview these men. But, although he got several letters from each and a tape recorded statement, they would not meet him. But they did give an amazing explanation as to why this had to be so. They said they were not ordinary police officers. In fact they were intelligence bodyguards who had a third person in the car with them. He was an important world figure whom they were taking to a heliport after a top secret meeting. En route their car engine and lights had suddenly failed and they cruised to a stop, ending up at just the right point to witness this abduction.

Given this, some felt that the experience must be a 'stage show' by the aliens specifically aimed at this world figure. He was meant to see it and others were meant to remember it so that they could support his story. Certainly, as of late 1992, that was the interpretation of the case Budd Hopkins appeared to be contemplating.

However, even if Richard and Dan were background figures they did visit Linda. Hopkins warned her they might do so. When they found she was expecting them this only reinforced their terror.

Hopkins claims that witnesses usually respond in horror to any proof that their abduction is real. For many it can only be lived with day in and day out if they persuade themselves that it was a vivid dream. The reality is too awful to contemplate.

But more surprises were to follow. Several other independent witnesses contacted Budd Hopkins during 1991 and 1992 explaining that they saw the UFO. During all of this the case was still not public knowledge, but more and more within UFOlogy knew of it. At least one woman crossing the Brooklyn Bridge claimed that her car and others were stalled by the UFO and that she saw Linda being floated out of the window. Hopkins eventually had three witness sketches of the abduction.

However, the case has its critics even from within the UFO

field. The disappearance of Richard and Dan poses a problem. Linda has reportedly alleged serious government harrassment. Some are concerned about the way things all fell neatly into the hands of Budd Hopkins in such a convenient manner, rather as I was concerned by the way I discovered so much about the events in Rendlesham Forest. I must also admit that when I saw the three witness sketches from different positions I was surprised that they showed similar perspectives. Hopkins has countered this in his reports and I should add that I have no doubts about his sincerity. I am sure he accepts the credibility of what he is reporting.

Perhaps it is merely that this case seems too good to be true, but time may well be the only thing that will tell if it is.

As for the identity of the 'third man', Hopkins and a few others know it. Hopkins even says he has a letter. However, that person is reputedly still not prepared to go public to explain what he saw. The time is not right. In September 1992 a UFOlogist revealed a name for this person at a lecture and this has since been repeated in several American UFO magazines. However, as no confirmation or denial has been made by the investigators or by the man in question, I am not going to repeat it here. But I will state that the name is indeed a world renowned person who has had strong connections with the United Nations, rather than being a head of any particular government. If he were to say that he had seen this abduction taking place it would be a significant news story.

As it is, once again the UFO world has been violently split by a major case. The truth, as always, remains in the shadows.

PART SIX

Why Are They Here?

Having spent some time looking at the claims, counter claims and hard evidence (such as it is) for the reality of alien contact it is time to ask what the point of all these strange visitations seems to be.

I realize that to do so may presume that 'they' really do exist. But for the purposes of this part of the book we will make that assumption, whilst remembering that there is a strong caveat to apply.

What I am reporting is a reflection merely of the stories themselves, not necessarily of any absolute truth behind these stories. You must evaluate them as you choose. Whether they represent any form of actuality remains an arguable question.

However, through a series of further case histories, we shall summarise the main reasons being offered by the aliens for the purpose of their visit to earth. Whether you regard any of these claims as fact, fiction, fantasy or something that at present is undefined, the words spoken during these hundreds of alien contacts are intriguing. Will we find that they all speak the same language and profess similar motivations? And will any of their messages provide new science, philosophy or knowledge that will teach us things about the universe?

Let us find out.

Souvenirs from Earth

It was August 1914 at Georgian Bay, Lake Ontario in Canada. A group of people on the beach noticed a most peculiar boat drifting off the shore.

In fact it was very unlike a boat, with a grey spherical body and a flat top. Around the middle was a band or ridge and upon this stood two small beings in purplish/green uniforms.

The tiny knot of people on the sands were puzzled by the antics of these youngsters as it was assumed that such strangers must be. A pipe or tube was being manipulated by them into the water and they seemed to be taking in liquid by siphoning it upwards.

At this point three other figures, also only about 4 feet tall, came from the top of the object. They wore khaki-coloured clothing and seemed intent on drawing the extended tubing back into their craft. After doing so the three men returned into the bowels of this floating craft.

One of the two remaining individuals stood on the rim of the object, completed the task of storing away the pipe and then followed his colleagues back inside, leaving just one of the small creatures alone on the edge. Before this one could descend inside the device the onlookers were startled to see that the UFO now took off skyward, finally dispelling all possibility that this was merely a strange boat.

The object tilted at an angle and flew away at speed with the stranded little entity clinging onto the side of the UFO as if his life depended upon it – which, if this story is true, it probably did.

Such a bizarre disappearing act has not been repeated since. Superficially it seems too absurd to be believed and was only told to American UFOlogists in 1966, well after the first alien contacts had surfaced. However, the image of beings who are oblivious to watching humans and only really concerned about sample gathering – in this case water – is a consistent one, particularly in some of the earlier alien contact cases. It is as if the collecting of souvenirs to take home to the stars is the point. But in 1966 that was, of course, exactly what we ourselves were in the process of doing on our first forays to the moon.

Water was a common alien target. For instance, in July 1919 at Webster City, Iowa, USA, a little figure scooped some into a can before rushing off into the landed object when spotted. He was bustled into the craft by another entity and this took off in such haste that it knocked branches off the tops of trees as it fled the scene.

Water was subject to several requests from aliens when they engaged in contact. Joe Simonton got his cardboard pancakes this way. It was also the start of the spring 1951 when an engineer was test-driving his car on the Draakensteen mountain near Paarl, South Africa.

The being in that instance was just under 5 feet tall and spoke in English with an odd accent. It approached the engineer, waving at him not to drive off home as he was intending and said: 'Have you any water?' After the man explained that he only had what was in the car's radiator, the entity repeated, 'We need water' and seemed to be rather desperate.

The engineer, interviewed by UFOlogist Cynthia Hind, reports how he took the entity in his car to a mountain stream, washed out an oil can, filled it with water and drove him back to a spot near a rock overhang. At no point had he expected to be confronted by a landed disk, nor to be invited on board this thing, but he was.

Inside the object several other small men were busy tending to one of their number on the ground. They totally ignored their guest; although this was (presumably) to them just as much an alien contact as it was for the human. The original entity did explain that their colleague had been burnt but refused the suggestion of a doctor.

A similar story befell a man at Santa Maria in Brazil in March 1954. He was met by two small and slim entities who carried a bottle with red liquid inside and reported that they needed ammonia. He was told that they came from a far distant star and their home was called 'Arion'. They had terrible weapons but ran away on contact with humans so as not to have to use them. But they were amused by the way in which earth people were so frightened when they stumbled across them. They were here on a purely scientific mission in order to take home plant samples.

Sampling of vegetation did indeed become a common theme after alien interest in water (or ammonia) subsided. We have already met cases such as Valensole, France, 1965, where lavender plants were taken by the small entities. This was typical of 1960s episodes.

Even in the 1970s sample gathering was often seen, although today it is very uncommon. A classic case from the Deeside area of Clwyd, North Wales, in July 1976 involved a girl who crouched behind a hedge for many minutes watching two small entities in silver suits wander around a field. One entity was digging holes with a ray-like implement.

Such seemingly pointless exercises are often found in these

close observation cases when there is no actual communication. It is one of the reasons why some researchers favour the 'stage show' hypothesis, suggesting that close encounters have another real purpose. They are to be watched by witnesses as if a play so they may conclude that these beings only take samples and have no hostile intent.

In nearly all of these 'souvenir hunter' contacts the entities are fairly human-like and slightly smaller than normal in height – 5 feet being typical. The same was true for the poachers beside the River Weaver in Cheshire in the January 1978 case where, if you recall, cows were studied and their measurements taken.

Passive interest in non-human earth fauna is often seen and, for some reason, dogs have created an intense fascination for the entities. They turn up again and again.

As we saw, they wanted to take the witness's dog from his home at Seddlescombe in Sussex but were placated by a china model instead. In the classic November 1980 Todmorden abduction police officer Alan Godfrey reported seeing a large black dog inside the UFO.

Other examples, of this extraterrestrial trade in 'hot' dogs are at Everittstown, New Jersey, USA, in November 1957 when a small entity told the witness 'we are peaceful people, we only want your dog' but was quickly chased away. And at Soria in Spain in 1978 where the entities told the witness that they were really only there to do a medical examination of his dog but they might as well take a look at him since he was there!

In Need of Repairs

Reg was an ambulance driver from Keighley in West Yorkshire when he met strangers from another world.

It was Febraury 1976 and he was resting in bed when he suddenly found some tall entities standing in his room, who seemed able to communicate with him via telepathy.

An image of a strange pipe or piece of bent tubing was projected into his mind along with the impression that their craft was broken and in need of repair. For some reason he concluded that they needed him to take a look and assist in this task so he mentally offered to do so.

He was made to lie prone on the bed, as if entering a catatonic trance, and then found that he was floating upwards rather like an out of body experience. He drifted through the ceiling as if it were not there and entered (he did not see how) an object akin to a giant bathtub.

Once inside Reg was made to lie on a table and inspected by a big eye-like device emitting a purple glow that probed over his body. He tried to ask what was happening but was told something about the Alpha and Omega and that he was an 'insignificant being' who 'like a worm' should not ask questions. But he was helpfully informed that to them time was different and a thousand of our years were 'but a day'.

All thought of the damaged tubing had disappeared and he later concluded that this must have been a ruse to put him at ease so that he would go with them willingly.

No hypnosis was carried out in this case and there was only sketchy recall but Reg simply woke up back on his bed, still paralysed and unable to move for some time.

This experience is typical of the way in which larger entities act, behaving more like ghosts than flesh and blood and with semi-magical abilities. Indeed it closely resembles the 'near death experience' and 'out of body' episodes of psychic research to an alarming degree, suggesting strongly that it was visionary in nature.

However, the image of aliens with stricken craft is one that has dominated the subject and is really just an extension of the 1954 Brazilian case where they needed ammonia to make their UFO fly again.

There does again seem to be a hint of a 'stage show', notably in cases such as one at the Stonehenge complex in New York where observers watched for hours whilst entities struggled to fix a damaged machine.

The same theme was also prevalent in some of the testimony about the infamous Rendlesham Forest landings in December 1980 outside the RAF base Woodbridge, Suffolk. Some of the USAF witnesses claim that the object that crashed down through the tree tops was damaged by the impact and that small entities suspended in shafts of light repaired the device before it took off again. Much of the other testimony from eyewitnesses does not support this scenario; although the presence of many military personnel surrounding an object on the ground after a crash landing and which eventually took off again is consistently reported.

Over the years, claims that UFOs have crashed to earth have

proliferated. The very first, in July 1947 at Roswell, New Mexico, is the only one to which UFOlogists attach much credence. Several books and a 1993 movie have been built around the testimony. Here, allegedly, the craft was caught in a storm and exploded into many fragments, but in later cases the device was said to be more intact on impact and sometimes captured, as were alien bodies (always of the small grey type).

Most of these 'faulty UFO' stories are rather dubious and are evenly spread throughout the years – up to and including the most recent in South Africa in 1989 where a UFO was supposedly downed by a space age laser canon fired at it. Investigation of this case, like most others, has failed to provide any real substantiation.

The number of UFO breakdowns in comparison to the total number of landing cases is far more than one might expect. If aliens are capable of building devices that achieve the seemingly impossible and bridge the trillions of miles of space between solar systems, then one must assume a level of sophistication that should preclude regular crashes, breakdowns in front of eyewitnesses and peculiar requests for spare parts from human watchers.

Again, speculation is that these must be 'set ups' designed to imply that aliens are not infallible and so make us less afraid of them.

The Tourist Trap

On 17 January 1974 a thirty-one year old man driving his car near Warneton on the Belgian border with France noticed his engine and lights faltering and then fading away altogether. His radio/cassette player ceased functioning as well.

Cruising to a halt the man tried to figure out what might be amiss when he caught sight of an object beside the road. This was like a soldier's helmet resting on legs.

However, he was soon to be distracted from this mystery, for coming towards him across the field were two decidedly odd creatures. Both had pasty grey faces and a small stature, not much over 4 feet in height. They also walked in a peculiar stiff gait. Their faces had pointed chins, creating a pear or light bulb shape to the head and only a slit mouth. They also had very rounded eyes. This was one of the earliest European sightings of the 'greys'.

The slightly taller of the two looked robotic in nature and had a glass dome on its head. The other beside him wore a Michelin man style suit formed of rolled material, making this a very similar figure to that seen in Bolton, Lancashire half a century before.

The figures stopped a few feet from the car and the witness felt a buzzing in the back of his skull and a sound that tickled his senses. However, the two beings just stared as if observing an exhibit in a zoo.

After an unknown period of time the entities swivelled around in response to a sound. This turned out to be an approaching car, at which point they reversed course and headed back toward the object. This took off skywards and disappeared.

The car stopped near the still terrified French driver. A man from a nearby Belgian village got out and asked if the witness was hurt. This second driver admitted that he had seen the entities and UFO and would come back to the scene with friends to seek proof. If they found any then he agreed to go fully public with the story. If not, the Belgian said, silence would follow. Evidently the outcome was the latter.

There are quite a number of cases on record where a witness is simply the subject of fascinated observation by the entities.

For instance, one of Britain's first alien contacts at Ranton, Staffordshire, in October 1954 involved a woman and her young children at an isolated farmhouse. They saw a disc-like object appear and hover above them with several of the Nordic-type entities (blue ski suits and long, blond hair). These gazed down from a window and watched the frightened humans with what was termed a mixture of compassion and sorrow. Despite this, witness Jessie Roestenberg took her children and hid under a table inside until the object had gone, with a purple flash of light – a response I think many of us would understand.

Indeed, Nordic type entities are commonly found in this kind of curious observation pattern – passing through an area and watching witnesses whilst remaining inside the UFO, rather like we might check out wild animals from our cars as we drive through a safari park.

In September 1977 a sixty-two year old woman, Ethel Field, taking in washing from her garden at Poole in Dorset, saw a dome-shaped craft float overhead emitting a powerful fuzzy blue glow. She shielded her eyes with outstretched palms and a few days later developed a skin disorder at a point where she says she felt 'heat' from the light emitted by the craft. Two silver suited entities were behind windows in the object and one of them was staring down at her and pointing, perhaps indicating her presence to the other. Ethel was not hanging about to find out and decided to rush inside and tell her husband and adult daughter who were watching TV. Sadly, they saw nothing unusual.

There was even a report from Sheffield, South Yorkshire, in March 1979 where a woman saw two blue-suited entities with long blond hair gaze down at her from a hovering UFO in what amounts to a virtual rerun of the Ranton case some twenty-five years before. Small details, such as the fuzzy blue or purple glow, were also repeated and this tempts one to think that the same object and crew were on some sort of galactic package tour taking in the sights of planet earth.

If so, the fact that a woman doing her washing or a block of shops in downtown Sheffield was of more interest than the Pyramids, Taj Mahal or Great Wall of China must provide some food for thought!

Universal Knowledge

Ashland, Nebraska, is a town in the deep mid-west of the USA, amidst the flat plains between Omaha and Lincoln where cattle roam, crops are grown and tornadoes occasionally wreak havoc.

In the early hours of 3 December 1967, twenty-two year old officer (later police chief) Herb Schirmer was patrolling in his car. At around 2.30 a.m. he checked on some livestock playing up and suddenly saw a dark object on the road ahead. He assumed it was a truck that had broken down. He switched on his spotlight and this illuminated a disc-like object on the roadway showing blinking lights. Grabbing a can of chemical spray used to deter attackers he edged the car closer. But the object took off.

At 3 a.m. he filed a report: 'Saw a flying saucer at junction of highways 6 and 63, believe it or not!' He was tired and unusually thirsty and also had a buzzing in the back of his neck and a peculiar red mark there. But he did not immediately realize that his timings were awry. Only during later investigation was it pointed out that fifteen or twenty minutes seemed to be unaccounted for.

The missing time was explored during several hypnosis sessions. Indeed Schirmer was one of the first to be so researched after the Hills story suggested this option. As a result a new sequence of events emerged.

When Schirmer shone his spotlight at the object it rose up and landed beside some electricity pylons. His car engine and lights had failed and his attempts to radio base for assistance also met with no reply. Then some small entities came towards the car. They were very familiar looking, under 5 feet tall with 'pasty' faces of grey/white, very thin lips and large cat-like eyes. A green mist covered the car and a beam of light was emitted by a hand held device operated by one of the figures. The patrolman lost consciousness, recovering outside his car talking to the beings.

They asked if he was 'the watchman' and he explained that he was. They enquired if there was a power station nearby or a reservoir. Then if he would shoot at their craft. Schirmer said not.

The officer was apparently led up into the object and given a vast amount of information in exchange for questions asked of him. They told him that this was an observation ship with four crew and that they had watched humans for a very long time.

They went into detail about how they operated in a vessel of pure magnesium, using 'reversible electro-magnetism' which affected gravity. They were sucking electricity from the overhead power lines to create a defensive force field used only when in proximity to the ground. This stopped engines and radios and created an ionization field. They even showed him a small object about the size of a car hub-cap which they said was a remote flying sensor that sent back pictures and which they despatched to check out an area before they landed.

As for their purpose in visiting, this was to collect animal samples. They referred to the fact that they had a 'breeding analysis' programme underway, but did not elaborate. This seemed to have been connected with human samples they were taking and is another early reference to the genetic experimentation programme which came to dominate later cases. In 1967 we were still struggling to make sense of the human genetic code.

In this fascinating case, Schirmer was also told that the aliens were concerned about our hostility – indeed that they had been shot at by military aircraft. They seemed intent on doing things to deliberately confound world powers who were trying to figure out their purpose. So they acted randomly when they knew that patterns and meanings would be sought. They could wipe us out, but that was not on their minds. Instead there was a long-term study project and Herb Schirmer himself would be revisited twice in future. However, they often prevented memory of the encounter, or just the contact aspect of it, so that only a very few witnesses had any recollection of what they were told, thinking only they had seen a UFO. There were huge numbers of hidden alien contacts.

In an intriguing statement, Schirmer was told that the point of all this subterfuge was that they intended that we 'believe in us some, but not too much.' In other words, the confusion, distortion, teasing nature of the evidence and so many of the contacts was very deliberate. It was meant to ensure that we were aware of their presence here but not in such an overt way that it interfered with their scientific mission.

Possibly one of the more remarkable things about the Ashland, Nebraska case is how it was duplicated in such detail thirteen years later. Then another young police officer in his patrol car was riding the streets at the edge of a country town in the early hours of the morning when he observed an object that seemed like a bus or truck. This case was the November 1980 Alan Godfrey encounter in Todmorden, West Yorkshire.

Some of the other weird connections are that Godfrey had also just checked upset livestock, then suffered engine, light and radio failure, was paralysed by a light beam, told inside the UFO that he would be visited again in future and lost a similar, relatively short, period of time.

In the 1951 Draakensteen Mountain case from South Africa (see page 137) the engineer was again given detailed information about the propulsion system of the object in exchange for questions he answered. He was told that they did not have engines but used a system that 'nullifies gravity'. A 'very heavy fluid' circulates in a tube and creates a magnetic field. But this fluid is subjected to radiation at the speed of light and so 'when the fluid is leaving the tube it is already entering at the other end ... its relative speed is infinite.'

Another case where specific information of this kind was offered is the October 1974 Aveley, Essex, abduction. Here a family of five were taken from the road in their car and had no memory of what took place except for vivid dreams and a conscious recall of driving through a bank of green mist (exactly as Herb Schirmer reported covering his car). The man and wife were both hypnotised and added a lot to their onboard experiences. In the husband's (John's) case this included a look at the UFO propulsion system and information about the alien mission on earth.

The long onboard experience was uncovered in hours of hypnosis (I attended one of Andy Collins' sessions) and it is intriguing trying to decipher the near magical nature of the supposed alien technology. Things were displayed and spoken which make little sense to us. Holes opened and closed miraculously in walls to create corridors out of nowhere and when a visor was explained the witness was told that normally the aliens 'see through your eyes' but 'when we cannot find suitable eyes we use the visor to change your lights to match our optic nerves ... It changes the impression that the static units on your planet see of us ... Static units are linear inhabitants.' It meant as little to John as it does to me.

This question of sight is interesting, because the Aveley witnesses noticed (as many others have) that there were very few colours in the UFO. It is often bland with light seeping out from all around. Being an artist John asked about this and was told that colours exist but do not seem to do so to our eyesight. Alien perception is different. It has also been implied that there are very dim light levels on their own world and this makes a great difference to when and how they could visit us.

The craft had two propulsion systems. An ion drive was used to travel in space, firing vortices of ionized particles. But this is very dangerous inside an atmosphere so they use an older method which converts the magnetic pole of particles surrounding the ship to the same polarity as that found inside the ship's core. This provides a thrust and a rapid cycling of this process creates the drive force. As a side effect it can also create visual distortions to the object when seen from the outside. This can provide invisibility, by filtering the light from objects surrounding the craft through a field and converting the data into a realistic hologram of the scenery whilst the craft is left unseen.

There was much more, but it was mostly just as incomprehensible.

His wife, Sue, learned a little about their breeding

programme. It seems that they have been watching us for at least 10,000 years and do not have children themselves: 'We reproduce through you. You are our children.'

Despite a wealth of information in cases such as these, there is rarely any specific indication of where the entities come from. They are not uncommonly asked where they are from and either point vaguely skywards or utter meaningless phrases like 'an outer galaxy' or 'far away'. Sometimes they utter silly names for a planet which sound like they come from a Dan Dare comic. At times one senses they have fun creating mystery in this way, or perhaps that the human mind – desperate for some origin – simply plucks these phrases out to ease the stress of not knowing.

Unfortunately, really useful information is very rarely offered to a witness; although there are two instances of supposed cures for cancer – both almost simultaneous in occurrence and many years ago. Neither have seemingly produced the sort of data that scientists could work with.

According to Brazilian doctor, Olavo Fontes, reporting to *Flying Saucer Review* in 1967, an unpublished case from ten years earlier (first reported on 14 May 1958) was of the following nature.

The daughter of a rich man in Rio de Janeiro contracted stomach cancer but, despite extensive treatment, in August 1957 they took her into the country at Petropolis hoping the air would ease her passing. On 25 October, while she lay in great pain despite morphine injections, a brilliant light lit the room and a disc hovered outside in the sky. From this emerged two figures about 4 feet tall with long blond hair and eyes slanted like those of a Chinese person.

The little group of people in the room of the stricken girl were amazed as the entities came into the house. One of the beings put his hand against the forehead of the girl's father and 'by telepathy' received details of her illness. They then moved over her stomach and this glowed with a blue light, exposing her insides like an X-ray. Pointing a small implement towards the cancerous tissue (looking like what we might now term a laser but which in 1957 did not exist) the being got to work. Some minutes later, as if satisfied, it stopped and the illumination ended. The young girl was now in a deep sleep.

The being then communicated in the same way as before that they would leave a small hollow object with the father. Inside were thirty tiny white balls. If they gave their daughter one a day for the next month she would recover. In exchange they were not to go public with this story. The family agreed, of course, and the girl did indeed fully recover, to the surprise of her doctors – who were not told what had happened.

The story was told by a servant of the family who was present, but she would offer no names. She said: 'I swear to you that everything really happened; my darling (Miss X) was condemned to die of cancer of the stomach and almost at the end she was saved by an instrument that looked like a flashlight that emitted some rays that took off the cancer ...'

A few other details were added, notably that the aliens reported that they came from Mars, were on earth to collect magnesium to build their craft and had carried out this cure, as they had made several other visits, so as 'to show us that we must have no fear of them'.

The second case happened in England and was reported immediately; although many details discovered during an investigation by UFOlogist Dr John Dale were not made public until years later. There can be no doubt that these two events are completely independent of one another.

Yet there are fascinating parallels. This case began only three weeks after the Petropolis event, on 18 November 1957, in a house at Aston, Birmingham. The witness, Cynthia Appleton, was a young mother married to a metal worker and with no interest in space or UFOs.

The entity involved was very similar (long blond hair and slanted eyes) – but 6 feet in height, typical of the Nordic cases. It did display the semi-magical nature found in the other case – eg., communicating by telepathy and also projecting holographic images (described with difficulty, of course, because in 1957 such things did not yet exist).

Several repeat visits followed over the next nine months, during which Mrs Appleton was 'educated' by the entities who came from a world they called 'Gharnasvarn'. She was told about the development of the laser – as used at Petropolis, perhaps – and gave details to Dr Dale before the laser was developed, let alone hand held surgery tools of years later.

Furthermore, her visitor made a point of telling her how to cure cancer. She did not even begin to understand; although Dr Dale recorded it as best as he could. The gist appears to be that it is supposedly the result of specific energy vibration changes in body organs that are in use at the precise moment when energy bathes the body. A change in the vibrational rate of sub-atomic particles occurs and they are permanently out of phase. The vibrational rate must be realigned by subjecting the body to a similar but reversed field.

Whatever the truth or nonsense of these claims, it is undeniably intriguing that both seem to be a great deal more logical in 1993 than they could possibly have done in 1957/58. At the very least, they were surprisingly advanced images of radiotherapy and laser surgery to 'burn away' cancerous tissue – uttered not by scientists, but as alleged words and deeds of aliens spoken via a young mother and a maid servant.

The Earth in Quarantine

On 24 April 1964 a twenty-six year old man, Gary Wilcox, was spreading manure on his land at Newark Valley, New York state, when an object appeared glinting in the sun ahead. So convinced was he that it was part of a plane that had fallen from the sky he went up and kicked it. He says that in texture it was like flexible metallic canvas.

As he was doing this two entities about 4 feet tall and dressed in all over white suits (that even covered their heads) appeared. They held a tray of alfalfa plants with roots and engaged in friendly chat for two hours, expressing interest in his farming methods. They even asked to take a bag of fertiliser and seemed intrigued by the idea of dead bones from animals contributing to the growth of new life.

In exchange they reported that they came from what we call Mars but humans could never visit as the atmosphere was far too thin (although in 1964 this fact was only dimly being perceived by space scientists). They also claimed that they had to stay away from city areas because the air was not pure enough and they had difficulty breathing even in country air.

The entities added that they were friendly and were studying earth but also sounded a note of caution. They warned that there was a coming change which would affect the gravity pull of our world and alter our environment. Our own pollution would not help. Indeed the earth itself could soon have an environment not unlike that on Mars.

In addition they suggested that a form of cosmic quarantine would doom humans from being able to travel into space and warned that the handful of Russians and Americans who had flown in earth orbit in the past three or four years would all die because of their journeys. This, of course, was a claim that was to be very quickly disproven.

Afterwards the entities returned into their egg-shaped device and it took off skywards. There are some interesting similarities here to the virtually simultaneous encounter involving police officer Lonnie Zamora in New Mexico – which followed ten hours later 2000 miles away.

The most interesting aspect of the Gary Wilcox case is its environmentalist message from a day when greenhouse effects, holes in the ozone layer and the need for urgent plans to save our biosphere were science-fiction tales that would have been taken no more seriously by most people than alien contacts are today.

Yet throughout the history of the phenomenon warning messages have been a significant feature.

During the 1950s these almost completely focused on the dangers of nuclear holocaust. Messages stating that the aliens were here to warn us that we were 'endangering the balance of the cosmos' by tinkering with forces we did not understand were commonplace. Of course, these reflected the anti-nuclear sentiments of protest movements and the underlying fear of humanity that these recently discovered weapons could destroy us all in the coming, all too predictable, war. As sociological phobias changed, so, to some extent, did the character of the alien warnings.

For instance, in July 1957 tall beings met a professor of law at Sao Sebasti, Brazil, saying that they had come to warn us about such dangers. But in July 1968 when Walter Rizzi was driving over the Grodner Pass in the Dolomites, northern Italy, his experience had a different theme.

Rizzi stopped to get some rest, but was awoken by a burning smell. Jumping out of the car he confronted a landed disc-like object and two beings about 5 feet tall with grey/green skins and hairless rounded heads. The eyes were slanted like a cat's and the nose and mouth just slits. Indeed they had many similarities with the greys of later cases.

A detailed conversation ensued, where the entities described (by telepathy) how they came from a 'distant galaxy'. They also reported that the green cast to their skin was not 'true' but that our perception of them was affected by 'the magnetic content of colour'. They travelled from star to star using a different propulsion method from that used on earth, which was a type of 'magnetic drive'.

This is something we have heard often before. For example, on 9 May 1985 a man on the East Lancashire Road at Lowton, Lancashire stopped his motorcycle for some tea at 4.30 a.m. and met two 5 feet tall entities with long blond hair. They reported that they came from the 'third solar system' and that their propulsion used 'the earth's own magnetic field and gravity' – but we would not comprehend any more than that.

However, Walter Rizzi was a bit more persistent in his questioning than that young biker. He asked why they did not openly assist us. The reply seemed to be that this overt activity was 'not allowed' and that our planetary conditions make them age very quickly so they have to limit their exposure on earth. Then came the warning, in reply to a question as to when we would become as advanced as they.

Never, Rizzi was told. Our planet has an unstable crust and its magnetic poles shift from time to time. In the very near future another such shift would be precipitated and as a consequence the geography and climate of the earth would change instantly. Eighty per cent of all life would be destroyed and the remaining humans would be confined to a narrow band of habitable land.

As the years progressed, pole shift stories became almost as common as nuclear holocaust warnings. In one case from Wiltshire, England, in 1977 where the entity materialised in a man's bedroom he was shown a 'hologram' – or 3-D image in space – to explain how this would occur.

A seemingly absurd alien warning saw the witness informed that our atom bombs were contributing to the imminence of the polar shift and that the aliens had a sort of 'glue' that they could inject into the cracks in the earth's crust to prevent such a catastrophe but they had not yet decided if it was appropriate to take this saving action.

This use of projected holograms of vivid reality – literally opening up in thin air before the witness like a living TV image without any screen – is a consistent part of the magical technology displayed during alien contact. It is frequently used for warning images – be they of the atomic, polar shift or increasingly common environmentalist variety.

The Cynthia Appleton case of 1957 is one of those which

featured such an effect before the invention of holograms and even today we have nothing like the sophistication these projections appear to possess.

In August 1971 two men had an interesting abduction experience when they encountered a thing like a giant 'brain' on the road and, mostly under hypnosis, one of them described an onboard experience with humanoid entities. Contact occurred by injecting a voice (which 'sounded as if it was the same voice I have to myself when I think') and a 'super advanced hologram' (as the witness described it in 1976).

The images were of atomic explosions in the polar regions and when the second witness was regressed he gave absurd prophecies (none of which came true). Even in 1971 these seemed bizarre. He asserted that the aliens had told him that world war three would begin in the mid 1980s but that all nuclear bombs dropped on the US would fail to explode. After the war, around 1987, the aliens would reveal themselves.

Contrast stories such as this with one from Edinburgh on 16 February 1980, where a thirty-nine year old man was woken in the night and went out to find an oval object hovering between the tower block flats in which he lived. This projected a beam of light which trapped him paralysed within the glow amidst a smell like sulphur. Three tall entities appeared, spoke into his mind and reported that 'this was our planet before you and we will not allow you to destroy it. If you try we will send a warning that will shudder the earth. Only the innocent will survive'!

In an even more extraordinary case a no-nonsense OAP in his seventies from Tetbury in Gloucestershire told me matter-of-factly how on 24 March 1988 he communicated with a UFO at the back of his garden. He went out trying to find a light seen from his kitchen window moving over the fields 'as if scanning' them, but failed to do so. However, as he was standing in the grass he was immersed in a beam. He cried out rhetorically 'what's going on!' and was surprised to hear a 'tinny' voice reply and lead him into a several minute long conversation.

He was told that they were 'just observing your world' and that the light he saw was 'a probe similar to how your scientists send out to observe other planets'. It contained no aliens. Instead, the voice was 'recorded on the probe and relayed to us'.

Then came the warning. He was told that we were 'gaining

knowledge so fast and getting to the very basis of the structure of matter and you could cause untold harm if you don't know what you are doing'. If we did not learn quickly they would 'have to take measures against you'. But they qualified this. It would not be very hostile. They would simply 'take action to reduce your activities ... You are very susceptible to bacteria and viruses. Something like that would cause disorganization ...'

The whole contact was a witty repartee (eg., when he asked where they came from and was told 'Ah well, you are not clever enough to understand that, are you?').

Fortunately, direct threats are virtually unknown – although the inference that we are tenants (in at least one case prisoners) marooned on this world is more frequently expressed.

But one of the most graphic uses of projected imagery was in the much researched Betty Andreasson Luca case from Massachusetts. Three books by investigator Ray Fowler have already been written exploring this single series of events.

It is interesting for a number of reasons, notably that the small greys seem to have immobilised and suspended in time the rest of Betty's family whilst they took her from her house. She went on a journey which has much in common with transformatory religious visions or cosmic purging where she visited strange realms, was put in tubes of fluid and shown images such as a giant bird – seemingly a phoenix-like symbol – possibly emphasizing the spiritual rebirth aspects found amidst this very unusual and complex set of close encounters.

In for Some Tests

Carl Higdon was a forty-one year old oil driller when he underwent an interesting alien contact.

On the late afternoon of 25 October 1974 he was hunting in the Medicine Bow National Forest Park near Rawlins, Wyoming, because he was unable to do the job planned for that day thanks to the unavailabilty of a co-worker. He had reached a spot where a herd of five elk were in his rifle sights when a very strange series of events unfolded.

He fired a bullet, but this 'floated' out of his gun and fell harmlessly to the ground. He felt the air tingle as if there were an electric storm. Then he was approached by a strange man, tall, wearing a black one-piece suit and with two horn-like rods on its head. Two rows of very prominent teeth dominated an otherwise slit mouth. Behind him was a cube-like object that was surprisingly small and into which the two of them together could not have fitted. Later he got the impression that space/time distortion was somehow involved in this.

The entity asked if he was hungry and then pointed a conical rod and 'floated' a packet with four pills into Carl's hands. Without questioning why, Higdon swallowed one and lost consciousness. He next awoke inside a room along with the five elk, who had apparently been captured.

There followed a very confused experience where the man was studied by a thing like a football helmet placed on his head and then taken on a flight in the UFO to what he was told was the aliens' world. There are some comparisons with the Betty Luca case and this was a very visionary experience, partly remembered right away but fleshed out later by hypnotic regression. It is quite possible that it was an hallucination of some sort, perhaps even one induced into him for a reason.

Either way he was told that we had a distorted view of time and that the trip (which lasted thirty minutes) was 163,000 light *miles long*. This is a meaningless statement (a light year, often misinterpreted as a duration, is actually the distance that light travels in a year – ie., billions of miles). Why would aliens make such an obvious error?

In response, Higdon says that this must be connected with the different interpretation of time and space, but similar astronomical absurdities have appeared in several other cases.

On this other world he was unable to cope because the lights hurt his eyes and the mistake was soon realized. He was advised that they had to stay in the shadows on earth during daytime for the same reason and wore clothing because our sun was too strong for them.

In what sounds like a story suited to the witness, the entity (who was called Ausso One!) said he was a hunter just like Higdon and they were visiting earth to take breeding stock back home for food because they could not sustain it without the earth's help. Interestingly, in a very similar line in another case, the witness was told that he did not know how lucky he was. The earth was one of the rare treasures of the universe being so full of myriad life forms which few other places could naturally sustain.

After his problem with the light Higdon was taken straight

back to earth and deposited some way from where he had started. His truck was 'moved' by the aliens into a muddy ditch, so that he had to radio for help to get out of the forest. It took some time for a rescue team (including the sheriff) to find him and he was still dazed with watering eyes when they arrived. He was taken into a local hospital for tests and released after two days recovering without the need for medication.

Carl Higdon claims that he was told that they had taken other humans before and were taking them in for tests but in his case these had shown him to be 'not good for their purposes'. He was left with the definite impression that at forty-one he was rather older than they wanted and, it is interesting to note, found himself wondering if the fact that he had had a vasectomy was in any way relevant.

There are other cases where peculiar tests seem to have been employed on witnesses. Interestingly these often feature repeat visits over a short space of time.

For example, twenty-seven year old Paulo Caetano told police of repeated meetings with small entities between 22 September and 19 December 1971 during which he was studied onboard. On one occasion he had to watch as an entity walked up and down a plank raised above the floor causing lights at each end to glow various colours as he went towards them.

Near Winchester, Hampshire, between November 1976 and March 1977 Joyce Bowles (on two occasions accompanied by a man named Ted Pratt) had encounters with bearded human-like figures from an egg-shaped object that was able to drag their car across the road.

On the first occasion, the figure simply went up to the car, put its hand on the roof and stared in at them, as if sizing them up. A month later (30 December 1976) they saw the object again when driving near Chilworth. The car began to rock from side to side amidst a high-pitched whistling. Then there was a memory gap and they were inside the object.

Three of the entities asked Ted Pratt to take some strides up and down the floor and were quizzical of how he felt after doing this. A number of things were said which were apparently indecipherable. At one point they were shown some transparent lines and symbols on the wall and it was suggested that these were 'fields'. Ted Pratt responded on the assumption the entities meant fields, as in grass, but they seemed rather perturbed by his failure to comprehend and said: 'No no no – *our* fields.'

Meanwhile, Joyce Bowles was giving as good as she got. Whilst her friend was being asked to report whether it was hot or cold inside the room she pointed out to the entities that their promise 'we have not come to invade you' did not amount to much. 'That's what Hitler said!' she told them – to which one being replied: 'You have a very strong tongue.' Deciding that she might have gone a bit far she said no more.

The encounter ended with a flash of light and the couple were back inside the car, unsure where they were. About an hour had been unaccounted for and – in the absence of hypnosis, which was not carried out – it is unsure how much memory remains unaccounted for.

In a later experience Joyce Bowles (with another woman this time) says she was given a message but that this was given to her mind and would not be revealed until the time was right.

A near identical theme appears in many other cases, particularly ones after about 1975. The Ilkley Moor abduction from December 1987 involved two holographic type films being shown which the witness will not discuss. One seems to have been of a personal nature and the other more connected with the environment. He was also shown images of the earth from space as if his reaction to this was of interest. From these cases it does seem that emotional responses are a source of alien curiosity.

Alien Rejects

Carl Higdon in Wyoming believed that he was rejected by the aliens who tested him. They told him that he was not suitable for their purposes – perhaps because he was too old at forty-one or because he had had a vasectomy to prevent him from fathering any more children. At least, so he thought.

There has been an undeniable series of references to breeding programmes, gynaecological testing, sperm sample-taking and such like from the very start of the abduction phase of these alien contacts. It is far and away the most consistent feature found in case after case all over the world. Indeed it has become so much a part of the phenomenon since the early 1970s that an abduction without reference to it is now rare enough to be commented upon by researchers.

Over the next three sections we will take a closer look at what does appear to be the overwhelming purpose offered for alien contact in almost all these modern cases. But what is equally interesting is that Higdon was merely one of the first – and certainly not the last – to be rejected by whatever tests are carried out during these encounters.

To tell a story that you are somehow not thought 'good enough' to be the subject of the alien scheme of things is a rather self-depreciating act. It does seem unlikely that we would have so many examples of alien rejects if the phenomenon were nothing more than wish fulfilment fantasy conjured up by imaginative individuals. Would they not far more likely see themselves 'singled out' as somehow important?

Indeed, even being accepted to be an active participant in this reputed alien medical programme seems not to carry with it the kind of ego-boosting story most people would be keen to relate. Rather it can be very demeaning. As such these cases do offer an intriguing undercurrent of reality that somewhat balances the occasional fanciful nature of the rest of the alien contact literature.

They certainly bring us back to earth – if only figuratively!

At 1.15 a.m. on 12 August 1983 a seventy-seven year old man, Alfred Burtoo, was fishing beside the Basingstoke Canal near Aldershot, Hampshire.

Burtoo was quite a character, having spent time out in the Canadian wilds braving wolves and others terrors. He was unusually fearless given his advancing years. On his way to his favoured spot, carrying refreshment from his wife and accompanied by his dog, he stopped for a chat with a stranger. This could have been anybody at that hour but turned out to be a patrolling officer from the nearby Ministry of Defence establishment.

Burtoo poured out some tea from his vacuum flask and proceeded to watch the water for any sign of fish nibbling at his bait. But he was distracted by a brilliant light which at first he assumed was a helicopter coming in to land. However, he realized how low it was and that it was curiously rounded. It descended gently onto the tow path some distance away and then the light went out.

Puzzled by this, he continued to watch as two figures approached through the gloom. His dog had seen them and begun to snarl. As they reached him he could see that they were small, perhaps 4½ feet tall, wearing greenish overalls and with visors over their faces. They gestured him to follow, so he set down his drink and left his dog (which had now calmed right down) and just went with them, merely intrigued to know what was going on. When asked later about this odd behaviour he reported that 'at my age you don't worry about these things. You can only die once.'

As he got towards the object he could see that it was much too wide for the narrow path and hung partially over the water's edge. A series of steps led inside and he followed the entities willingly. He had to stoop down to enter as the ceiling was only inches taller than he was. There was no attempt at collusion nor fear on the part of Burtoo.

Inside the rounded object was a hexagonal corridor. In the centre was a column about 4 feet wide that went up to the roof. As one of the beings stood by the door (perhaps barring the exit) the other spoke in faltering English: 'Come and stand under the amber light.'

The fisherman only saw this light when he moved towards the column. But he considered there was no harm in standing there and did so. He was then asked to give his age, and proudly announced this as seventy-eight next birthday. Then he was told to turn around and face the wall. He saw and felt nothing as he did so, but waited there some minutes, before the voice announced: 'You can go. You are too old and infirm for our purpose.'

He was led out of the craft and walked some distance away before turning round to see it climbing silently upwards, the top part rotating as it did so. He went back to find his dog acting as normal and his tea cold. But he still drank it. He had considered UFOs 'bunk' before, but now knew differently. Upon arrival home he immediately told his wife.

It is interesting how well the Burtoo and Higdon stories fit; although one finds it difficult to understand why after thirty years of supposed testing such a mistake as this could be made once more.

Then again, in Brazil on 15 October 1979, a mother of seven and a concert pianist (Luli Oswald), was driving on a coastal road between Niteroi and Saquarema with a twenty-five year old male friend of one of her sons. It was late at night and although they saw some odd lights there was no further conscious memory, but there was an unexplained two hour time loss on the drive and Luli had serious physical after effects (e.g., eye trouble and an inability to urinate for forty-eight hours).

Regression hypnosis revealed a deeper 'memory' of being inside an 'operating room' with small grey-skinned creatures with ugly features akin to a rat. These sound similar to the ones that carried out the medical examination (under supervision from taller Nordic type humanoids) in the 1974 Aveley abduction from England. However, Ms Oswald did comment that they may have been wearing unusual clothing and masks to produce the rat-like impression.

The woman had hair samples taken and was then given a gynaecological examination. During this she saw her friend on a table nearby stretched out and pale as if dead. She was informed that, being a young man he was suitable and they were intending to 'keep' him but that she – very much his senior in years – would be returned and was of no use to them.

Luli recalls seeing some transparent tubes taking blood from the man but no more until they were both back on the road after the time lapse. She was told by the entities that several groups are on earth – including one from the poles – and some do not mind what they do to humans. He was different and came from 'a small galaxy near Neptune' – a phrase she was intelligent enough to see was nonsensical. Of her memory under hypnosis she remarked that it was awful because 'It isn't real, but it happened all the same'.

An even more intriguing 'rejection' case is that of retired teacher's resource centre manager, Elsie Oakensen, whose calm and rational account of her November 1978 encounter has proven very influential since she has bravely gone public with her story. She has helped many recent witnesses to such things come to terms with their experience via a sort of self-help group in London.

I recount this case in some detail in my book *Abduction* and Elsie has also written her own book (yet to be published) – with the delightfully apt title of *Why me*?

Essentially she was driving home from work when she observed an object which, given the circumstances, hundreds of others should have seen but seemingly did not. Then on a quiet road into the village of Church Stowe, Northamptonshire, she lost all power and lights on her car. She was surrounded by a strange pulsing flash and recovered further down the road, the car now functioning normally but with about fifteen minutes unaccounted for.

She was regressed once some time later to try to plug the gap, but this met with limited success and I asked her to attempt another altered consciousness technique (creative visualization) at the exact spot of the encounter, so duplicating the original event. From a combination of these processes she reported how she felt, that she was scanned by a bright light and led to an isolated spot. She dimly perceived 'grey shapes' moving about but felt that the scan had led her to be rejected and so she was returned to normal consciousness some way further down the lane.

What is probably more important than any of this is that there was a completely independent sighting less than two hours after Elsie's encounter and only four miles away.

Four women, younger than Mrs Oakensen but who did not know of her or her story (and vice versa) were driving through the village of Preston Capes. They saw similar coloured lights to those which first alerted Elsie Oakensen and then parallel beams shoot from a cloud. Their car began to lose power and the object paced them, until they entered the village lit by streetlamps and the car returned to normal. The UFO lights now merged into one and vanished.

Unfortunately, at the time nobody knew there was a clear link with Mrs Oakensen's experience (indeed at the precise time of this second sighting she had even reported a tightening band sensation around her head similar to one felt before and during her earlier encounter). Consequently, nobody really looked for deeper possibilities in the Preston Capes sighting – eg., exploring whether there was a time lapse or whether any of these women had unusual dreams or after affects.

Nine years later I tracked down the driver of the car, who would not put me in touch with the other women. She seemed to know nothing of Elsie Oakensen's story (which was not to attain any real publicity until after this interview). The driver of the second car confirmed that it had only been a few months old and had never given trouble before or since. However, she clearly considered the incident best forgotten and made apparent that she did not wish to talk further about it.

To me these events in Northamptonshire on that November might may be crucial to our knowledge of this phenomenon. Knowing Elsie as I do I would endorse her sincerity completely. I also have no reason to doubt the credibility of the second story. Yet taken together they appear to preclude all possibilities but one – that some intelligent source was on the lookout for a contact that night and, having tested Elsie and found her unsuitable, almost immediately homed in on another prime target – four younger women alone in a car on a nearby quiet road.

Whether the outcome of that was, as conscious testimony suggests, just another distant inspection by the lights, or whether there is a hidden dimension to that case (or indeed a third more successful contact later that night) we may never know. But it is hard to see coincidence as the only factor in these events, just as it is difficult not to see a frightening consistent logic in stories of alien rejection.

The Genetic Experiment

In November 1983 on my first visit to the USA I met UFO abduction specialist Budd Hopkins at a conference in Nebraska. Late one night he suggested that a little group of us, including Dr J Allen Hynek, retreat to a back room at the university complex to hear of an amazing new case that he was starting to research. I tape recorded a lengthy impromptu presentation of these events, unaware that the episode was set to become a story that would eventually become world famous in UFO lore. Indeed, in 1992 the events would inspire a major networked TV mini-series based on Hopkins' book – 'Intruders'.

In fact, for some time I was rather embarrassed by having this tape and kept its existence to myself, because the witness had insisted upon the use of a pseudonym and Budd, in his typical friendly and cooperative manner, had shared with his colleagues all details, including the woman's real name. As such I had a tape which, for a time at least, newshounds would have paid well to hear but which, of course, I had no intention of sharing with them.

Eventually, the woman in question chose to break her given pseudonym (Kathie Davies) and go public under her real name (Debbie Tomey). So I now feel unrestricted by the existence of this tape. It certainly allows confirmation of a number of claims that can be dated to a time when such matters were of much less obvious significance than they had already become by 1987 when Hopkins' work was published after Strieber's *Communion*.

Debbie Tomey began a lifetime of strange experiences at the age of seven when she met an unusual 'little boy' who 'played a trick on her' which involved a cut to her leg. This left a scar. Other incidents followed which registered little in the conscious sense but were later explored by Hopkins under hypnotic regression.

The key to these seem to have been a series of events in 1977 and 1978 (when Debbie was aged eighteen and nineteen). Here she had at least two experiences of being taken into a UFO and medically probed. On the first occasion she was floated up from out of her car and on the second taken from her sister's home. Both of these involved gynaecological probes. The third also featured a small implement supposedly put up her nose and 'implanted', creating what at the time was an inexplicable heavy nosebleed.

In the examination Debbie reported how she felt her stomach being squeezed and her legs pulled – sensations not at all dissimilar to the account by one of the three women from Telford, Shropshire in 1981.

A graphic description followed of something being placed inside Debbie and a suction device in operation. There was no real pain throughout any of this and she noted the similarities with pelvic examinations during later pregnancies.

In early 1985 Debbie first told Budd Hopkins that she believed she had had an alien child as a result of these onboard experiments. The entities had shown 'her' to Debbie (it was a girl) during an abduction in October 1983. The child looked about four years old and was beautiful 'like an elf' with thin white hair, the large eyes and egg-shaped head of the greys but a somewhat more human appearance. She was led to believe that this was a hybrid that had been conceived by her, then extracted from her womb at an early stage and 'born' in the aliens' own environment. Indeed, Debbie confessed, since her 1978 abudction she had had some bizarre 'dreams' of a super-intelligent and odd-looking baby.

These 'wise baby' dreams were something Hopkins now sought in other female abductees and was soon surprised to discover they were not rare.

The entities involved in all of Debbie's abductions were the typical 4½ feet tall large headed ones so common in American UFO lore – the greys.

Of course, with the summer 1987 publication of *Intruders* any pretence that there was no contamination was lost to the data. Witnesses now had access to Hopkins' book and surrounding publicity (and later to media appearances by Debbie Tomey and others) and so were clearly well aware of the details of what occurred during the alleged gynaecological experiments and the creation of the 'wise baby' hybrids.

Nevertheless, prior to 1987 at least, this phenomenon was unknown even to UFO researchers such as myself. We did have a fairly uncontaminated period for case collection. Any sign of such things within the records are very important and it is quite astonishing to see to what extent this does emerge from a study of the evidence. Often these cases had no publicity outside rare sources within UFOlogy or, indeed, not uncommonly, no publication at all prior to 1987.

Here are just some of the clues that emerge:

In August 1965 at San Pedro de los Altos in Venezuela a respected gynaecologist was visited by tall Nordic beings with large round eyes. They gave the usual nonsensical spiel about coming 'from Orion' but added that they were 'studying the possibility of inter-breeding with you to create a new species'. However, they warned that there were also smaller entities (seemingly the greys) who were actively kidnapping humans and who had less certain motivations. These beings came from another silly origin – 'the outer dipper'.

In May 1968 a nineteen year old nurse's aide was taken from her home in New York State and returned with strange red marks on her abdomen. She stopped menstruating for nearly a year and after a while went to a doctor, and then a gynaecologist in Uttica. Nobody could work out what the problem was but just under five years after her initial abduction she returned to normal. Under hypnosis (in January 1975) she recalled being medically examined by small figures with off-white skin, pear shaped heads, large eyes and no hair. Ova samples were extracted through a long needle and she was told that they had selected her to give them a baby which they could experiment with. 'We are studying [you] ... we want to see if we can [have a child],' they advised.

In October 1973 at Langton Buddville in Somerset a woman in

her car was stopped by a UFO and taken into a room where she was medically probed by beings with large round eyes. She gave great detail about the procedures. She was naked. The room was cold like a fridge. A pencil-like object was probed around her body and nail and blood samples extracted. Then a device was placed over her vagina and she felt a sucking sensation and ova were extracted. All this was consciously remembered. She was too scared to be hypnotised and afraid of her husband's reaction.

In January 1976, in a case remarkably similar to the Telford abduction five years later, three women in a car were abducted together at Stanford, Kentucky. The two older ones (aged forty-four and forty-eight) seem to have just been observed by the usual small entities. But the youngest (who was then thirty-five) was put on a table and felt her bones being twisted and something entering her stomach and 'blowing up' inside. A full gynaecological survey involved suction (of ova samples) from her body.

Later in the 1970s a young woman was taken up into a UFO from somewhere in northern England and placed on a table. I have been asked to be no more specific to protect her identity, but she was medically examined by entities with large eyes, pale skins and very blond hair and recalls her feet being pulled and probed. After the experience she began to have strange dreams and became unexpectedly pregnant but a few weeks later she found blood on her bedclothes and was no longer pregnant. It was presumed that she had had a miscarriage but she is adamant that she could not have been pregnant in the first place as she did not have a boyfriend. This was reported long before Hopkins first published details of his 'wise baby' or 'hybrid baby' cases in America but has never been reported by me, given the woman's sensitivity on the matter.

In 1980 a young woman was driving her car in the early hours of the morning in a remote area of Finland. A sudden mist enveloped the car and she found herself inside a room being medically probed on a bed. A gynaecological examination was conducted and she was told by the small entities of the standard 'grey' type that they could not 'beget children' and so needed her assistance.

* * *

In mid 1984 a woman from Cheshire had the strangest in a series of experiences which began in summer 1979 with a close encounter sighting of a UFO. Weeks later she had become unexpectedly pregnant and then had a series of dreams (which she discussed with others) where she saw the baby born, looking ugly and having an incredible intelligence. So scared was she by these recurring nightmares that when, three months into the pregnancy, on 26 December 1979, she saw blood on her clothes and was told that she must have miscarried she was glad. Four and a half years later in August 1984 she heard the same humming noise that accompanied her 1979 UFO sighting and awoke in the middle of the night to be floated through her bedroom window by a tall, blonde female entity with large blue eyes. All she recalls of her experience inside the UFO (largely forgotten and never explored under hypnosis due to a self imposed ban on such matters by British investigators) was of being studied and knowing that something 'very important' had occurred. Three years later, in April 1987, she awoke to feel tiny fingers touching her own but only has a dim recall of what happened next. She is convinced that a child of two or three years of age was holding her hand. She called out to her husband who switched on the light. As he did so she saw a ball of light rise out of the room. All of this was reported to me, and had no publicity, before I saw pre-publication details of Hopkins' work on wise baby and alien hybrid cases in the USA. The young woman in Cheshire could not possibly have known about such things and at no time even connected her dreams, miscarriage or the subsequent 'tiny baby in the bedroom' with her UFO experiences.

The threads weave together in a remarkable way. The pattern that emerges is disturbingly simple and yet utterly consistent. If there is no underlying reality why should this be the case – indeed how could this be the case?

Synthesis

A worrying pattern seems to emerge from the evidence and must be accounted for by any explanation that we propose. Of course, it is true that some witnesses must be fabricating stories, for whatever reasons, and that in other cases there are psychological forces looming large. But I believe that the inter-relationships between these reports is one reason why we cannot deny them all.

A synthesis of the long term trends comes through the evidence, but where do we go from here?

We cannot know how far folklore stories about 'other beings' relate, if they relate at all, to alien contact of this present century. It is worth continuing to research such options, but we will always be unsure whether myths and legends are simply that or have any basis in reality. So it is unwise to draw too many conclusions.

However, the records of what are said to be actual eyewitness accounts do feature two consistent types of entity – the small 'greys' and the tall 'Nordics' that have dominated the literature. That is not to say that no other entity types have been reported. As you will have seen, they have. But they are very much the exceptions.

There was at first a noticeable geographical spread – with the Nordics appearing far more in Europe and the grey beings almost entirely American based, but this has changed somewhat since the early 1980s. Now there are more greys seen in Europe and less Nordics altogether. On the other hand many British cases have been a sort of intermediary between these two extremes with characteristics of the two. Because American abduction cases get far more publicity than any other around the world (and indeed because there are a lot more of these cases owing to the widespread use of hypnosis there and not elsewhere) the image of the grey has been imposed upon the world as the standard latterday alien.

These differences occur, however much American researchers prefer to wish them away, suggesting that if British or Australian researchers distrusted hypnosis less than they do, then such a 'screen memory' of more pleasant entities would vanish and the reality of the greys would shine through.

Of course, this is simply what they hope would happen. The geographical difference in entity types is a major negative factor against their literal reality, perhaps implying a sort of visionary experience where culture is reflected in the precise nature of what is seen. Indeed, changes since the worldwide publication of many images of the 'greys' in books such as *Communion* and *Intruders* even further supports that idea;

otherwise why would greys suddenly dominate countries where they were formerly quite scarce?

A similar worry appears with alien warning messages, which have adapted over the decades – from anti-nuclear to environmental – as if to mirror our own concerns rather too closely. Some researchers say that there is a correlation in the other direction, it exists because human concerns (from CND marches in the 1950s to green policies of the 1990s) have been inspired on a subconscious level by the intervention of aliens. Well, perhaps! How on earth does one disprove that?

Certainly, the earliest alien contacts were quite simple – entities tended to avoid any relationship with humans and were often deliberate in their attempts to prevent this when caught unawares. A witness would be rendered unconscious whilst the entities got on with inspecting rocks. The method of ensuring that they were not disturbed was interestingly consistent, given the 'ray gun' imagery of science-fiction. Just as the dominance of monsters in 1940s and 1950s fiction had almost no impact on real alien contact stories, so alien weapons have been rather more simple than ray guns; pencil like devices rendering paralysis.

The same was true over the next decade or so when alien activity seemed to centre on taking plant samples and a curiosity with biological specimens (eg., dogs and cows seem to have been a peculiar attraction). Again a witness was usually immobilised whilst they just got on with their activities.

An important consideration is that we now have so many years of contact with supposedly alien technology that we can examine it for what has been called 'cultural tracking'.

If you imagine a time traveller from 1943 looking at our technology of 1993 there would be much that would bamboozle. They would be left bemused by video recorders, home computers, holograms, lasers, microwave ovens, indeed quite a lot of things we use every day.

This should have two consequences for alien technology, where we are in the position of that time traveller. Firstly, alien technology should not be static and ought to develop with time. Secondly, there should be consistent features about it which mean more to us today, given our greater knowledge, than they did in the past – but which were described in cases half a century ago just as they are described in cases today.

What do we find? Cultural tracking is undoubtedly there in some cases. Early abductees spoke of huge machinery on board UFOs with levers and dials. These are less common today.

This is all a bit like looking at the two series of the 'Star Trek' TV shows made over twenty years apart. The 1960s 'Starship Enterprise' used designs that seemed futuristic in 1966, yet still had dials that clicked around from number to number because nobody could predict that very shortly we would all be using LED displays (or numbers created by light beams as on all equipment today). This is only one of the examples of a small but significant change in our technology in just a short time. The new 'Star Trek' series had to be set decades into its future partly so as to adapt what was already antiquated technology by our 1980s standards into one that seemed science-fictional. There is little doubt that twenty years from now it too will look equally archaic.

These lessons are critical to the reality of alien contact, because if sightings were simply imaginary in some form or another they would display this 'Starship Enterprise' effect. If instead we have always been observing a real alien technology and struggling to describe what we see then this effect would, on the other hand, probably not be present. Indeed, this may be one of the best ways to resolve the question of imagination versus literal alien reality.

Can we answer this vital question?

In a Brazilian case reported as it happened in 1957 and one of the earliest accounts of entry inside a UFO the witness described a 'lift shaft' that sucked him up into the UFO and how once inside everything was lit by an 'extraordinary light' that had no obvious source. The room itself was devoid of much instrumentation but there were windows and doors appearing in the walls which from outside did not seem to be there.

In a 1967 Nebraska case the same strange illumination featured and there was a viewscreen 'like a TV set' with a switch that flipped up and down. A catwalk encircled the UFO.

The Aveley abduction occurred in 1974 and the witnesses here also saw a catwalk around the UFO. Again there was a sort of view screen upon which images like holograms were displayed. Witnesses again referred to the illumination which had no obvious source. Doors and windows opened up magically in the walls and resealed as if they had never been there.

Moving to the detailed description of the UFO in the

December 1987 Ilkley abduction, here again the strange lighting from nowhere is a source of puzzlement to the witness – indeed he comments on this several times. He is shown a screen that emerges out of a wall as if it is part of it and shows realistic images which are like 3-D holograms.

As you can see there are mystifying features that recur in these cases and do not seem to have been affected by the passage of time. These include the peculiar ambient illumination, the way in which doors and windows appear seamless and the 3-D holographic TV screen (found in at least one case from before the concept of holograms, 3-D images and before TV sets were widely used). Such things do tend to support a basically stable and seemingly alien technology.

However, there are also anachronisms, such as the large computers found in older cases and the way in which some UFOs have steps leading up to them when in others aliens 'float' or suck the witness up in a beam or shaft. Consistencies undoubtedly outweigh the inconsistencies, but not to such an extent that one can be absolutely sure of one's ground. As so often it is like taking one step forward and another step back.

We have already noted the use of hand held laser implements looking like pencils – which were used in the 1957 cancer cure case and regularly ever since. Indeed the technology of the medical examinations during the years has been remarkably constant – featuring illuminated scanners passed over bodies well before we had similar devices in our hospitals and the quite astonishing use of tubes to suction off ova samples well before we had test-tube baby techniques.

On the other hand, why would alien technology duplicate our own? Would not a civilization that does things that we cannot imagine – such as crossing the vastness of space – have better means of extracting genetic material than an incredibly cumbersome experiment involving the repeated medical sampling over decades of time? Unless, of course, the experiment requires such interaction with humans over a long-term basis?

There have been other impressive points that emerge in these cases – which I call the 'pink frog' indicator. Just as many alien contacts share essential storylines, so many cars look alike. If we want to decide whether two people have seen the same car the fact that it sports something very unusual and unlikely to be commonplace (eg., a pink frog hanging in the back window) could be the key to establish identification.

We have seen such a pink frog indicator on several occasions. For instance, the repeated reference to the unusually large eyes of the entities and, whenever this is discussed during a contact, the claim that this is because of the lower light levels on their home world. Indeed, on earth, animals adapted to live in low light conditions often have very large eyes. Add to this cases where entities are said to deliberately avoid direct exposure to sunlight or stay within the shadows, even the fact that alien contacts are much more prevalent at night than during the day. Lots of little clues such as these all seem to slot together.

There are more direct links. In the Schirmer case from Nebraska in 1967 the witness was told about miniature devices used by the aliens to feed data back and help decide where to land. Years later, a man in Gloucestershire, whom I am reasonably certain knew nothing of this American case, had a contact with what sounds exactly like the device that Schirmer was told about.

Such interweaving patterns are not uncommon and, for obvious reasons, UFOlogists are loathe to reveal too many of them because, once in print, their value as a reality check becomes diluted.

Just as one further illustration, look at how often entities refer to two types of propulsion system, one for use in inter-stellar flight and another only whilst in the earth's atmosphere. The latter virtually always consists of a device that harnesses the magnetic field.

Indeed, there are now enough cases where details have been offered that, coupled with the extraordinarily consistent interference effects to car engine and lighting systems, a physicist could probably decode the material to determine if anything of scientific sense emerges. Perhaps it would not, but I merely note that these cases are not full of wide-ranging pseudo-science as might be dreamt up by vivid imaginations. Instead they reflect a curious and regular pattern. That pattern may reflect some reality or it may be arrant nonsense, but it is a pattern nevertheless.

Clearly, the alien contact stories went through a dramatic change after the rock and plant sampling era. Suddenly, witnesses became the focus of the episode. Both consciously and via hypnosis they would report being taken against their will inside a UFO and from the very start how the purpose seemed to be to conduct a medical examination. The genetic experiment that was supposedly involved in this process established itself very quickly and it is most uncommon for an abduction case not to include a medical examination and practically unheard of within the records for such an examination not to have some seemingly gynaecological, sexual or genetic aspect.

Indeed, this pattern may well be the most significant of all. For there are clear signs that even in the years between 1957 and 1965 when the first cases had occurred but had yet to be published there were events taking place with hints of these things coming through.

Again, if we were dealing with widespread imagination in the wake of these first abduction cases one would have expected a big range of stories where the person who is imagining is often in control or emerges in some way as a hero of the experience. But the person is instead always subjected to terrible trauma, emerging with a series of repressed memories equivalent to victims of rape. These are not the kind of stories you would expect from some wish fulfilment fantasy sweeping the world.

If we look at the contactee cases from the early 1950s and compare them with the abduction evidence from the last three decades the differences could not be more marked.

Contactees were almost invariably men, interested in mysticism or outer space, who claim to have been singled out by generally benevolent and very human-like aliens with a very simple philosophy of peace and love. The contactee was often engaged in some form of act that elevated their status (eg., going to the moon, being earth's representative in some other worldly United Nations and even saving the solar system from destruction like an intergalactic Indiana Jones!). They created groups around them, collected acolytes, published treatises, gave lectures and enjoyed touring the world trying to bring their story and its message to the people.

As for abductees today, there are at least as many women as men (in some studies women outnumber men two to one) and they cover a wide spectrum of society, often having no interest in space or mysticism. The aliens are usually at best indifferent, not infrequently do things that are at least psychologically stressful and rarely offer any kind of philosophy or even answer questions that are posed. Rather than being singled out as some special earth emissary for wiser beings the abductees feel as if they are victims of an unspeakable crime and certainly wish the events had never happened to them (something hardly any contactee has ever suggested). Abductees shun the world, only one in ten (on best estimates) reporting their story. Even then they are painfully afraid of going public – in some cases to the extent of not telling husbands, wives or close family, let alone going on some global crusade.

These glaring differences may prove very important. At the least they suggest that the two sets of stories may not have the same origin. They could well represent how alien contact might manifest in both a romantic fashion as well as some rather less desirable actuality.

Of course, set against all of this we face the problem of the physical evidence – or rather the almost complete lack of it.

Abductees are almost never seen during the abduction and even then there is zero evidence that they ever went anywhere.

Photographic evidence is almost nil, despite a massive increase in camera ownership, widespread use of video camcorders and better film that can take pictures at night. There are even few attempted fake photographs of alien contact; although this would, of course, involve rather more effort than throwing an ash tray or hub cap into the sky!

Even when the aliens provide proof of themselves – in the form of things ranging from crystals to implants inside the body – this has upon investigation the calibre of Joe Simonton's cardboard pancakes.

Why is this? Of course, one conclusion might well be the most obvious; that alien contacts never really happen; witnesses only think that they do. But this has to be set against the evidence suggesting that they are very consistent.

A further speculation has been that 'they' (the aliens) control the amount of proof that we are allowed to see (remember Herb Schirmer being told 'you should believe in us some, but not too much'). If this is the answer, then the appearance since 1987 of those few dramatic cases which seem to escalate the level of proof to unprecedented heights may represent a very dramatic new phase of activity.

If it does, then where is it leading us to?

PART SEVEN

Conclusions:
What is Going On?

This is not a book with answers. My purpose has been only to present a review of the evidence for alien contact – from the basic stories to the solid proof (such as there is of it) and from the claims given to witnesses by the alleged entities to the frightening logic of what might turn out to be an alien genetic experiment.

What you choose to believe about all of this material is, of course, up to you. You must balance the often contradictory evidence against itself and try to decide upon a reasonable outcome.

This is far from straightforward and may even be impossible under present circumstances. But I hope that you will realize that increased levels of research are desperately called for and that, whilst it is always easy to scoff and presume these cases must be nonsense, this is just the quick way out. It does nothing to shed light on such a puzzling phenomenon. That requires rather more effort.

If only one or two scientists, philosophers, or dedicated individuals wake up to the fact that there are no simple answers to what is certainly a far more intractable problem than they imagine, then this book will have done its job.

But it seems appropriate to leave you with a brief digest of some of the key contenders presently being considered by those who are braving ridicule and attempting to resolve this mystery. One of these solutions may prove correct. Or that elusive answer may be something as yet undreamt of.

Time, or, perhaps as some would hope, a mass alien landing, may one day tell!

'It's all in the mind'

Most people are reluctant to ascribe the hundreds, if not thousands, of alien contacts to the result of hoaxing. There are undoubtedly some hoaxes, but these often stand out from the rest. However, any motive for widespread trickery is far from obvious. These witnesses are overwhelmingly unlikely to seek publicity or to gain in any way from their stories. A few do, of course, but they are clearly the exceptions.

So, the next most obvious proposal is that the stories are all imaginary in nature – perhaps a fantasy desire for other intelligences to talk to us, borne out of what researcher Paul Devereux aptly calls humanity's 'cry of a lonely species'.

Some evidence fits this well. The lack of solid support for the actuality of the experiences is one thing. But we also have the way in which some people during alien contact have been clearly observed and went nowhere (certainly not inside a UFO). They are, as a consequence, simply imagining (or more correctly 'imaging') that they have done so.

However, if it is as simple as all this, we have major problems to account for. Experiments have been carried out to attempt to show that witnesses are what psychologists term 'fantasy prone', ie., they have such vivid imaginations that they cannot distinguish reality from imagination at certain times. All of these psychological experiments, now several of them, have failed to support the fantasy prone hypothesis, to the extent that at a seminar to discuss such results in June 1992 one of the pioneers of the idea, Australian case worker Keith Basterfield, publicly withdrew the theory from consideration.

Witnesses have been found to be of above average intelligence, creatively visual but also of a wide cross-section of the population. They are undoubtedly convinced of the reality of their experience to the extent that it has a serious detrimental effect on their well-being. Whatever they may be, these are not wish fulfilment fantasies, according to all psychological reports from those who have studied the question.

Similarly, Dr Eddie Bullard, an American folklorist, has tried very hard to show that abduction stories adapt with time as folklore does. But his work into hundreds of cases (easily the most in-depth ever carried out) has utterly failed to support this view. He has no answers.

'A mystery of the psyche'

The so-called 'psycho-social' hypothesis has strong hold in Europe but is derided by researchers in the USA. It is really a more advanced version of the 'all in the mind' concept and so suffers from the problems of that theory.

The experiences are perceived as waking dreams acted out like psycho-dramas by the consciousness of the witness in response to some inner stimulus.

In all of us dreams occur in the same way, mental images shuffled whilst we are in an altered state of consciousness (sleep) and acting out plays that reflect things that are of importance to us. Some dreams can be remarkably vivid, called 'lucid dreams', where the dreamer actually knows that it is a dream and can to some extent control the action.

One idea is that alien contacts are like lucid dreams occurring in a non-sleep situation i.e., when the witness is in an altered state of consciousness yet, technically, or according to most definitions, being 'awake' rather than 'asleep'. The drama that results is in response to inner tensions (everything from phobias about nuclear war to repressed memories of child abuse have been proposed and researched with so far no substantial evidence). Quite why it would always take the form of alien contact and not, for instance, miraculous transportation to a desert island, is unclear; although the way in which this may be an update of an age old experience where previously the aliens were seen as fairies or other worldly spirits might offer suggestive evidence.

Some psychologists have noted the similarity between somnabulistic (sleep walking) states and narcolepsy (where a person experiences brief loss of consciousness whilst 'awake', often without realizing). It is suggested that people prone to such things in the presence of a UFO stimulus might lose consciousness (perhaps because of the tension bringing on this latent condition) and 'dream' something of relevance to their last memory before this period of unconsciousness. If that last memory were of a UFO the resultant dream may well then be of subsequent alien contact 'filling out' their impression of what would happen next.

Again no experimental evidence exists to support such theories.

'Super humans?'

The fact has been noted that many who claim alien contacts also have a track record of other psychic experiences (eg., seeing ghosts, having out of body experiences, etc.). From this some do now speculate that alien contact may simply be another expression of a peculiar talent that certain human beings possess.

Just as in some cases people can 'tune in' to alleged past lives and describe in remarkable detail what these entail, or a medium can 'pick up' messages from deceased individuals, so too may alien contact witnesses enter an altered state and somehow 'commune' with another intelligence.

It is not necessary to believe that past lives are real or that the dead actually live on to acknowledge that these phenomena occur and require some solution. The same applies to the alien contact. Real contact at the level of consciousness may happen, but so may some peculiarity of the way the brain decodes information. All this theory can say with assurance is that these abnormal consciousness experiences do happen on a visionary level rather than one that occurs within literal reality. The trigger for the vision or communion is harder to evaluate.

There is support for this. These encounters appear to involve a shift in the state of consciousness of the witness, noted as the Oz factor at the onset of an event. Also the phenomena seen are rarely witnessed by others at the site who should have been observers had it been an event outside the consciousness of the witness. Similarly, we can note how alien contact often occurs in a way described by witnesses as 'telepathic' or frequently happens when the mind is already in a form of altered state, such as in bed late at night, or on a lonely road whilst driving a car.

Psychologist Dr Kenneth Ring, from the University of Connecticut is one of those who has seen the parallels between alien contacts and near death experiences (where people see a bright light and wise beings but interpret this as a limbo state between life and death not a meeting with a UFO and extraterrestrial). He wonders if both might not be reflections of a form of super-consciousness emerging in a few individuals who act as heralds of an evolutionary shift towards a new kind of human being. Indeed, alien contact witnesses are in many ways rather like the shamans found in less technocratic cultures.

'A mind scrambling mystery'

Many UFO researchers accept that reports are a 'catch all' for a diversity of phenomena, ranging from up to 95 per cent mistaken identity for mundane things (eg., aircraft, balloons, stars, etc.) to new atmospheric phenomena not yet fully understood by science.

A range of research projects have continued to uncover clear evidence that there are natural phenomena associated with atmospheric vortices, electrical processes generated by stresses in rocks and microwave emissions which can create free-floating glowing balls. When seen these could well be interpreted as alien craft and are, by definition, 'unidentified objects that are flying'; that is, UFOs. The support for at least two, perhaps more, so called UAP (unidentified atmospheric phenomena) is strong and growing. Much laboratory and experimental research has been conducted and both geophysical 'earthlights' and electrified 'plasma vortices' have been successfully produced under controlled conditions by scientists in Britain, the USA and Japan.

Going further there is also strong evidence (from research by neurophysiologists) that certain energy emissions can stimulate the cortex of the brain and trigger realistic hallucinations even in people not prone to such things.

It has been speculated that very close contact with a UAP (which a witness would today evaluate as a UFO and, by social context, probably as an alien craft) may trigger such hallucinations as a result of emersion within radiated energies. The outcome would be physiological effects (and from experiment these do match those often claimed by alien contact witnesses to some degree) plus an hallucination. As the witness is placed into a stressed situation by the real perception of a genuine phenomenon they would very possibly hallucinate an alien contact under these circumstances and, of course, would pass psychological tests (eg., lie detectors) because the phenomenon first encountered was real.

In a few cases, such as the 1980 Todmorden abduction, other witnesses have seen 'lights' but nothing further in the area where an abduction was experienced by the person in closest contact. This, very possibly, was a UAP.

'The multi-dimensional approach'

The consistencies between these events suggest to some that an intelligence is behind them. But what of the long-term nature of the encounters or how they fit in with cultural beliefs of the relevant era (basically from the little people of old to today's little green men)?

Perhaps all of these experiences throughout the history of mankind result from contact with a mischievous race that co-exists on earth and which presently is happy to play to our belief that they are alien visitors. But this interpretation is no more valid than was the concept of fairy lore or clever airship inventors in the last century.

It is interesting to note how the entities in alien contacts often distort the truth. Their origins are almost always astronomically absurd and they frequently tell witnesses things that make no sense, such as referring to light years as a time rather than as a distance. It seems that these confabulations are deliberate and may be meant to amuse or confuse, certainly they appear to imply that the entities' origin is extraterrestrial when in reality it might well be no such thing.

We have no way of judging the response to human beings of a hypothetical species that co-exists on earth possessing intelligence and language, clear emotions, even self sacrifice, and having an organized society. In fact there really *is* at least one such intelligence. It is called the dolphin.

If we have no way of comprehending dolphin society but are aware of its presence, how might they react to us? Dolphins live in another 'world' – the sea – and presumably can have little idea that on land is an amazing civilization of biped beings who build cities and have wondrous technology. Only very occasionally do we interact with the dolphin world when we leave our environment and enter theirs.

Equally, another form of intelligence co-existing on earth may do so in an intriguingly analogous way. Would we be sporadically aware of the intrusions of a mysterious intelligent race from a realm beyond our reach (except when they take us into it)? Such hypothetical compatriots of ours might exist in a so far unexplored dimension that science is only now beginning to comprehend as a possibility. It may exist around us all the time (according to our growing knowledge of space-time physics). Would these beings treat us rather like we treat dolphins?

'Back from the future'

The similarities between human beings and aliens are biologically worrying. There seems no good reason why an alien life form would not be as different from us as we are from the dolphins. Yet, according to the testimony, people never have contact with extraterrestrial giraffes or get abducted by elephantine creatures from *zeta reticulii*.

In science-fiction the common way out of this problem (caused by the saving on make-up and special effect budgets) is that a human-like race colonized the galaxy millenia ago and so we are all related in some way. Perhaps so, but there is something disturbingly human about these alien contacts, not only in their appearance but also behaviour. Surely real aliens would have a psychology that was incomprehensible to us?

One suggested way out of this is the idea that alien contacts are, in fact, visits by beings from our own future. In other words our descendants literally coming back from the future to look at us. In this way they would appear and act like us. It is just as we might appear were we to go back and study Neanderthals. Would they not see us as extremely clever and possessing amazing technology but nonetheless similar in appearance and very human in behaviour?

If we did travel back in time to visit primitive humans we are unlikely to say, 'Hi – we are your future descendants'. More likely we would study them, take samples, go back home and do experiments and let the beings conclude whatever it was they wished to conclude about us (very probably that we were 'sky gods'). Legends would blossom and we might well even take a perverse pleasure in pandering to those legends.

We have no way of knowing whether time travel will ever be a scientific possibility (but some physicists regard it as less improbable now than they did before our knowledge of quantum mechanics developed). If we ever do perfect it – even hundreds or thousands of years from now – presumably future humans would occasionally visit our time. In other words, if we see no evidence today that time travellers come here it proves that time travel is forever impossible. But if it is not impossible we should see evidence that travellers are here and have been visiting throughout history. The alien contact evidence can readily be adapted to fit this possibility. But it is, of course, just another theory.

'ET has landed'

Undeniably the most popular way to interpret the evidence is to take it at face value and assume that we are really being studied by aliens from another star. But scientists reject the evidence because they simply cannot accept this as an explanation. They seem unwilling to familiarise themselves with any other possibilities. Partly that is because the media endlessly repeat this false logic that UFOs are spacecraft. You must either believe in ET, or UFOs do not exist. You now realize that this is quite incorrect but it has become such an engrained truism within our culture that it is hard to escape from its clutches.

Oddly, scientists do not reject the existence of aliens. There are billions of stars and the evidence strongly points to many of them having planets and at least some of these having developed life. Indeed NASA is so convinced that they are out there it spends huge sums of money trying to pick up radio signals hopefully sent out by these beings. They are using radio – a technology we have had for less than a century and which is next to useless to communicate from star to star. If you sent a radio message to the nearest possible ET intelligence it would be nearly ten years before you got an answer. If you tried to contact most alien planets the wait would be hundreds of years!

Our technology is streaking ahead. Only 100 years ago our best hope of contacting aliens was the serious proposal of using giant mirrors to flash out coded messages. Today we have radio. Tomorrow, who knows what we may have discovered or invented that will be infinitely superior to this ET equivalent of the carrier pigeon.

Despite this fundamental flaw, science is so keen to contact aliens that it ignores the drawbacks and spends vast sums whilst at the same time openly ridiculing the evidence presented in this book. If ever there were a case of double standards, this is it. It is just to be hoped that the error does not prove prohibitively expensive.

Whether or not real alien contact is the answer to the riddles that are in this book, it is obvious to anyone who thinks about it for a moment that researching the possiblity would cost a fraction of what it does to scan the universe for radio messages. There can be no good reason to continue to neglect full investigation of these alien contact cases.

Generally, the argument as to why scientists reject the evidence (with which almost none of them are familiar) is that travel to earth by aliens is impossible because of the limitations of space. The restrictions imposed by Einsteinian physics prevent travel at the speed of light and make travel at significant fractions of this velocity so difficult that it is widely regarded as impossible. This combines to make interstellar flight both incredibly expensive and prohibitively long (journeys would take thousands of years at best).

Of course, all of this suffers from the myopic perspective of present day science which says that because we cannot think of how to do it nobody else ever will. The same view was uttered about travel beyond 100 MPH at one time in the not so distant past and space flight to the moon was called 'bilge' by a top astronomer not much more than a decade before it happened!

So this is a rather dubious argument to cling to; although it is one that should not be ignored entirely. It does go a little deeper than simply saying we can't do it so nobody can. It relates to the way in which we interpret the laws of the universe. But we have underestimated those in the past, so it is wise not to be too adamant that space will have no loopholes which make what look like impossible voyages today become a pretty easy hop at some point in the future.

However, even if space travel is impossible, this does not rule out the ET hypothesis. There is evidence that these alien contacts are visionary in nature and we have seen other problems associated with the interpretation of these experiences as actual landings by alien craft. We cannot rule that possibility out, but aliens might also have a way of communicating across great distances that is far quicker than radio waves and which we fail to comprehend. If that probe could home in on people on earth and trigger a visionary contact, perhaps draining out information in some form of consciousness to consciousness interaction across the light years, then how would we experience the event? Would it be as a baffling, confusing and contradictory alien contact, the reality of which we are struggling to understand? In other words, do they even need to come here at all to make extraterrestrial contact possible?

References

Readers may find the following sources referred to in the text to be of value in their search for further information. Several have subsequent editions, including some foreign translations. Both new and out of print UFO titles are available from special sources listed below.

The Interrupted Journey; Fuller, John, Dial Press, New York 1966 (An updated version with extra transcripts appeared from Souvenir, 1982).

The Humanoids; edited by Bowen, Charles Neville Spearman, 1969.

The Mothman Prophecies; Keel, John, New American Library 1976 (A new version of this classic book is now available via Enigma Design).

The Hynek UFO Report; Hynek, Professor J Allen, Dell, New York, 1977.

The Walton Experience; Walton, Travis, Berkeley, 1978 (Reissued and retitled *Fire in the Sky*, 1993).

Missing Time; Hopkins, Budd, Marek, New York, 1982.

Close Encounter at Livingston; Campbell, Steuart, BUFORA, 1982.

UFO Dynamics; Schwarz, Dr Eric, Rainbow, USA, 1983.

Communion; Streiber, Whitley, William Morrow, 1987.

Intruders; Hopkins, Budd, Random House, 1987.

Melbourne Episode; Haines, Dr Richard, LDA Press, USA, 1988.

UFO Abductions: A dangerous game; Klass, Philip, Prometheus, USA, 1989.

Perspectives; Spencer, John, MacDonald/Futura, 1989.

Abduction; Randles, Jenny, Robert Hale, 1989. (An American edition, entitled *Alien Abductions* available from Inner Light, New Jersey, 1990).

The Gulf Breeze Sightings; Walters, Ed and Frances, Bantam, 1990.

The Watchers; Fowler, Ray, Bantam, USA (only) 1990.

The Aveley Abduction; UFOIN Case report by Collins, Andrew and King, Barry available in edited mimeograph, 1991, from Enigma Design.

Scary Stories; Hough, Peter & Randles, Jenny, MacDonald/Futura, 1991.

Scary Stories; Hough, Peter & Randles, Jenny, MacDonald/Futura, 1991.

UFO Crash at Roswell; Randle, Kevin & Schmitt, Don, Avon, USA 1992.

Secret Life; Jacobs, Dr David, Simon & Schuster, 1992 (Fourth Estate, London, 1993).

The Omega Project; Ring, Dr Kenneth, William Morrow, 1992.

The UFO Encyclopedia; Clark, Jerome, Omnigraphics, USA 1992/1993 (A massive three volume set of superb historical research material).

From out of the Blue; Randles, Jenny, Berkeley, USA, 1993.

Crop Circles: A Mystery Solved; Randles, Jenny & Fuller, Paul, Robert Hale (Updated edition, 1993).

The proceedings of the June 1992 symposium on UFO abductions that was held at MIT (Massachussets Institute of Technology) are scheduled to be published in 1993 and will be indispensable reading. They have over 100 papers and half a million words penned by international specialists examining the alien contact from every conceivable aspect. Check with specialist booksellers for availability.

You can keep up to date on current happenings and new cases through the following sources:

BUFORA (British UFO Research Association) publishes *UFO Times* magazine, Suite 1, 2C Leyton Road, Harpenden, Hertfordshire, England AL5 2TL.

Also operates a weekly news and information service (UFO Call), written and presented by Jenny Randles, and available throughout the UK at current 0898 line rates (45p per minute peak time as of 1.9.93).

Call: 0898 12 18 86

Both Northern UFO News and UFO Brigantia, issued separately but with a unique joint and reduced subscription deal, focus on new European UFO activity. Copies are available (along with many UFO journals from the USA and special offers on otherwise hard to trace new publications) from:

Enigma Design, 15 Rydal Street, Burnley, Lancashire, England BB10 1HS.

The independent magazine *Flying Saucer Review* often carries translations of obscure overseas cases, eg., from South America, and is available on quarterly subscription only from:

FSR Publications, PO Box 12, Snodland, Kent ME6 5JZ.

Important American magazines which have detailed studies of new cases are:

International UFO Reporter (from the J Allen Hynek Center for UFO

Studies) 2457 West Peterson Avenue, Chicago IL 60659 USA.
MUFON Journal (from the Mutual UFO Network)
103 Oldtowne Road, Seguin TX 78155-4099 USA.
In Australia there are regular updates from UFORA (UFO Research
    Australia) at: PO Box 229, Prospect, South Australia, 5082.
Books can be obtained from specialist sellers or by mail order from
    the following. Those marked * primarily offer second-hand
    bargains.
Arcturus Books, 1443 SE Port St Lucie Boulvd, Port St Lucie FL
    34952 USA.
Lionel Beer Books, 115 Hollybush Lane, Hampton, Middlesex TW12
    2QY.
*Midnight Books, 21 Windsor Mead, Sidford, Sidmouth, Devon,
    EX10 9SJ.
S Stebbing Books, 41 Terminus Drive, Beltinge, Herne Bay, Kent,
    CT6 6PR.
*Sydney Esoteric Books, 475-9 Elizabeth Street, Surry Hills, NSW
    2010, Australia.

*   *   *

Reders wishing to report any personal experiences can contact the
    author (in confidence if preferred) c/o 37 Heathbank Road,
    Stockport, Cheshire SK3 0UP.

Index

190 INDEX